Charter Schools:
The Parent's Complete Guide

Charter Schools: The Parent's Complete Guide

Everything You Need to Know to Make the Right Decision for Your Child

Frederick A. Birkett, Ed.M.

PRIMA PUBLISHING
3000 Lava Ridge Court · Roseville, California 95661
(800) 632-8676 · www.primalifestyles.com

Every effort has been made to make this book complete and accurate as of the date of publication. In a time of rapid change, however, it is difficult to ensure that all information is entirely up-to-date. Although the publisher and author cannot be liable for any inaccuracies or omissions in this book, they are always grateful for corrections and suggestions for improvement.

PRIMA PUBLISHING and colophon are trademarks of Prima Communications Inc., registered with the United States Patent and Trademark Office.

Library of Congress Cataloging-in-Publication Data
Birkett, Frederick A.
    Charter schools: the parent's complete guide : everything you
need to know to make the right decision for your child /
Frederick A. Birkett.
        p. cm.
    Includes index.
    ISBN 0-7615-2516-5
    1. Charter schools—United States. 2. School choice—United
States. I. Title.
LB2806.36.B47 2000   00-060654
371.01—dc21

00 01 02 03 HH 10 9 8 7 6 5 4 3 2 1
Printed in the United States of America

HOW TO ORDER
Single copies may be ordered from Prima Publishing, 3000 Lava Ridge Court, Roseville, CA 95661; telephone (800) 632-8676, ext. 4444. Quantity discounts are also available. On your letterhead, include information concerning the intended use of the books and the number of books you wish to purchase.

Visit us online at www.primalifestyles.com

CONTENTS

Purpose and Plan of the Book

I AM THE DIRECTOR of an elementary school dedicated to the success of its students. We—the staff members of Benjamin Banneker Charter School in Cambridge, Massachusetts—expect to meet the educational needs of the children placed in our hands. If you understand that, you can probably imagine my disappointment when a parent fairly new to our school came to tell me that she had chosen the wrong school for her child. As she tried to explain why she felt as she did, she repeatedly compared Banneker School with a school that her child had attended before. This woman had a rather clear idea of what she wanted and expected from a school. And, had she and I talked before she enrolled her child at Banneker, I could have warned her that her ideas and our program did not match very well.

This parent—a sincere and well-intentioned woman—made what she considered a mistake because she was unaware of simple steps she could take to determine *before* she enrolled her child whether Banneker was the kind of school she wanted for her son.

As she departed, I was left thinking about her situation. I realized that many parents with a choice of schools find themselves making an unfamiliar decision. Under the circumstances, they do not know how to go about making a wise decision. Yet the steps are fairly simple, and the information that parents need is neither difficult to obtain nor complex.

When I looked for information to address the needs of parents considering placing a child in a charter school, I could find nothing on the market. The few books available about charter schools are research oriented, written by university researchers and professors who look at schools from an academic point of view rather than a practical one. These books primarily presented comparative and statistical studies. They didn't offer the practical information parents need.

At that point, I decided to write this book.

Purpose of the Book

THIS BOOK WILL guide parents who are considering placing children in charter schools. The need for this guide arises from "the choice movement" and the rapid increase in the number of charter schools across the United States. For me, this book is very personal, growing out of my position as a charter school director. During the past four years, I've interacted with several hundred parents who've enrolled their children in charter schools. During my day-to-day interactions with these parents, it's become apparent to me that many considering charter schools don't understand fully what charter schools can and cannot do for their children. I realize that many parents, though delighted with an opportunity to exercise choice, don't really know how to make the best choice for their children and for themselves.

As the parent of a school-age child, you have the right to information about your child's educational options. But if you aren't aware that this is your right, or you don't know what questions to ask, or you don't understand the kinds of answers you get when you do ask questions, then this guide has been written for you.

I developed this guide most specifically for parents considering enrolling children in a charter school or parents choosing between two or more charter schools. The process and ideas presented here, however, will also be useful to any parent evaluating any school option for his or her child.

If you are a parent considering whether to move your child or children into a charter school, the book you are holding can become your roadmap to a successful journey. I look forward to traveling with you.

School Choice Movement

THIS GUIDE IS timely. Recently, education has been a major agenda item for political candidates from the president of the United States on down. It's a key issue with political candidates because it's number one in the hearts and minds of Americans. The public's concern with education comes from a growing and widespread realization—now fifteen years in the making—that many public schools are failing our children.

The school choice movement, particularly the rapid development of charter schools in the United States, arose from this public concern. The idea of choice has a strong American flavor and obvious appeal. The wealthy have always enjoyed the privilege of selecting schools for their children. Some choose schools that meet particular needs for the child or the family or both. Family convenience is often a consideration— a school close to home, a school close to work, a school with extended hours, or even a school with boarding arrangements. Others choose programs to enhance a child's special talent—a strong performing arts program or strength in modern or classical languages. Some select schools based on educational philosophy and approach—a disciplined atmosphere as opposed to open classrooms. Some want a demanding, challenging academic program to meet the needs of a particular child and a gentler, more nurturing environment for another child. And some choose schools to maintain family traditions. These are all legitimate preferences and considerations for some families.

Concerns About Public Schools

DESPITE THE APPEAL of choice, few of us go looking for alternative schools if the neighborhood public school seems to be meeting all of our children's needs. If you are reading this book, there is a fairly good chance you are less than happy with the public school serving your family and children.

Parents are drawn to charter schools for several important reasons. Of course educational quality, the soundness of the education provided by the local public school, is a key concern. Writing for *Reason Magazine* in January of 2000, author Michael Lynch illustrated this concern with the story of a Washington, D.C., grandparent, Bernice Gates. In 1997, Ms. Gates had struck a deal with her then seventh-grade grandson Silky. He was to tutor his younger brother Derek. The deal broke down when it turned out that the seventh grader, who was getting good grades at the local public school, was working at a level below his third grade brother who was attending a small, private church school.

Like Ms. Gates, you may be concerned about educational quality. Research indicates that many students enter third grade unable to read and write. This fact alone frightens many parents and prompts them to question whether their children are in the right schools and whether their schools can provide top-notch educations. Some parents may wonder if their children are going to graduate without being able to read the words printed on their own diplomas.

In addition to quality education, parents are also concerned about safety. With the rash of school shootings during the past several years, the safety of children is on the minds of every single parent who sends his or her child off to school every morning. If your children are stuck in large, overcrowded schools and classrooms, you may be concerned for both their education and their safety.

Other parents have more specific or personal concerns with the local public school. In some cases, their children have had a history of academic failure. Parents of children with special needs often wonder if an alternative school could serve them better. This is often as true when the special need is for a greater challenge as when the need is for more support. Parents who've encountered disagreements with the local school over appropriate disciplinary procedures for their children also sometimes seek alternative educational arrangements.

But running through all of these concerns is yet another common problem many parents face with much of the current public school system in the United States. That problem involves a lack of respect for and a lack of responsiveness to parents. In addition to a strong education for her grandsons, Ms. Gates was looking for a school administration that would return her phone calls, answer her questions, and keep her up to date on her children's progress.

On the face of it, these expectations seem like a given. One might assume parents in most public schools normally experience a basic level of respect and responsiveness. But having had personal experience with traditional public schools where administrators and teachers didn't respect my knowledge as a parent about the best approaches for meeting my children's needs, I am familiar with the frustration that Ms. Gates felt.

My own experience convinces me that many public schools don't value the wealth of knowledge and information parents bring to the arena. Instead, too many administrators and teachers ignore or pacify parents concerned about their children's education, proclaiming that they are the professionals who know better than parents what's best for children. Too many traditional public schools consider parents a necessary nuisance, best avoided if at all possible.

If you are unhappy with your local public school for any reason, an option like a charter school can seem very attractive. *Charter Schools: The Parent's Complete Guide* was written for all the Bernice Gateses of the United States who are trying to find schools that will provide their children with quality education and better futures and will treat parents themselves with respect. This guide is also written for parents who are seeking schools that employ innovative approaches to education, that move away from the approaches that leave many students unmotivated and indifferent.

The traditional public school system does not give parents much credit for being able to distinguish one school from the next. And minority parents are singled out as not knowing what is best for their children academically. In fact, alarmed at the spread of school choice programs, spokespeople for teachers' unions and others have suggested that the low-income and minority parents, whose children are primary beneficiaries of such programs, tend to lack the necessary background or motivation to make sound education decisions. Some believe parents will end up basing their choice of school not on academic excellence or discipline but on factors like sports teams or proximity to home (Finn, 1999).

The charter school movement does create options for families of very modest means. The theory behind the movement hinges on the conviction that putting parents in charge is the surest, perhaps the only, way to raise successful kids, shore up our weakened families, and cure our ailing education system. Parents have their children's best interests at heart more than any government official or paid official or paid professional ever could; parents can be counted on to do the best they know how to do. If parents know how, they will be wise and conscientious in their choices.

Making the Right Choice

BUT WITH CHOICE comes a new responsibility. To choose wisely, you need information and knowledge. This book is for all parents determined to choose wisely and to separate effective schools from ineffective schools. Thus the purpose of this book is to help parents become wise consumers in the vast educational marketplace as they shop the public charter school market.

Charter schools vary considerably in size and in the population of students they serve. Grassroots parent and community leaders run some; private companies run others. Some make parent participation mandatory; others require very little involvement on the part of parents. Charter schools are better at meeting some needs than others; some charter schools can meet needs that others are not equipped to meet. How can you determine whether charter schools in general and one charter school in particular can give your child an appropriate education? I developed this guide to help you gather the information you must have to answer that question.

Charter Schools: The Parent's Complete Guide leads parents through a step-by-step process, explaining what to do, what things to look for, and what questions to ask when investigating the possibility of enrolling their children in a charter school. My guide provides parents with the kind of information that will equip them to be knowledgeable consumers when speaking to school administrators and teachers about their children's education. I explain how to get the information you need and how to make sense out of everything you see and hear as you investigate schools for your children.

I want to emphasize the need for you, a parent interested in school choice, to do a thorough investigation of the school in which you're thinking of enrolling your child. The bottom line is not what the school says it's going to do for students generally, but what it can do for your individual child. Many schools claim they can solve the educational problems of all children who enter their doors. Check the school out before you check your child in.

You need to understand the different kinds of school programs that are out there. Your ability to understand these differences will allow you to find the right school for your child.

Although charter schools by their very nature attempt to be sensitive to the needs of their constituents or customers, they nevertheless face many of the same problems as all other schools, public, private, or charter. Charter schools employ human beings, with all the blemishes that go along with being human. The schools will end up with some teachers who cannot teach, some parents who are not as involved in their children's education as they should be, and some students who are not engaged in the learning process.

Charters schools, however, do appear to be making a difference in the lives of many children and families. Many parents polled have expressed the pleasure they have had in seeing their children with a new sense of educational purpose and a love of learning they never had before. Many children in charter schools express feelings of being appreciated and cared for. Charter schools in general are doing a superb job of animating the stakeholders in their immediate communities. Students are re-engaged; they feel safe, and they are interested in learning. Parents are grateful. So, while the jury is still out on whether charter schools have fully accomplished what they set out to do, the results look promising.

One benefit of the school choice movement is that more and more parents are waking up to the fact that they have choices when looking for the right school for their children. Many of these parents are realizing they don't have to feel as if their children are stuck in schools that are physically dangerous, allow low performance, have inadequate facilities, provide poorly trained teachers, and deliver an unmotivated student body.

Choosing to place your child in a charter school will give you an opportunity to become involved in your child's education to a large extent—or to a lesser extent. This will be up to you and the school in which you choose to enroll your child. Remember, by enrolling your child in a charter school you will have an opportunity to make a difference in the type and quality of education your child receives. It will be an opportunity to be involved in shaping the education you believe is best for your child.

But I must tell you up front that, ultimately, sending your children to a charter school won't really matter if you don't provide them with the necessary support they'll need at home—the kind of support that reinforces what a child learns in the classroom. In the final analysis, it doesn't matter how great the charter school is or how innovative the teachers are. What ultimately matters is how hard your child works and how much support, guidance, and encouragement he or she gets from you in the process.

The Pages Ahead

THE CHAPTERS ARE organized to provide you with a structure and approach for understanding and judging any school you visit or consider for your children. The book carries you through a logical exploration of charter schools as an alternative to your local public school. In addition, the appendixes provide a range of resource and supplementary information for your use.

Chapter 1 explains what a charter school is. Charter schools are compared with other public schools and with private schools. I provide a clear definition of the whole charter school concept, explaining how it came into existence, the laws governing them, the benefits, and the concerns.

Chapter 2 focuses on helping parents understand the essential importance of a charter school's mission and purpose. This chapter introduces some basic concepts that make up educational philosophy: curriculum, instruction, and assessment. By reading this chapter, you will be able to identify your own educational philosophy and start the process of determining if a school's particular philosophy aligns with your point of view about your children's needs.

In chapter 3, I lay out the actual activities a parent will need to undertake to judge any particular charter school—or any school, for that matter. Who will you need to talk to? What documents will you need to read? Where do you need to go and when? Because one of your first steps will involve a meeting with the school director, I explain how to evaluate the leadership of any school you consider.

Chapter 4 focuses on a school's curriculum and standards. I define for parents how important a solid curriculum and high standards are in providing an adequate education to children. I also point out what to look for in a school's curriculum, such as content, and whether it meets state standards.

I explain in chapter 5 more about instruction, teaching, and teachers. I look at different teaching and learning styles. I stress the importance of quality teachers, and I encourage parents to gain a full understanding of various teaching and learning styles to determine what styles meet the educational needs of their particular children.

Chapter 6 clarifies the purposes and methods of assessment. I explain the importance of measurement and assessment to the student, to the teacher, to the school, and to the educational system responsible for overseeing schools.

Chapter 7 explores three important charter school constituencies—each with a major role to play in the governance and decision making for charter schools. These groups are the school's own board, the state chartering agency, and, above all, the parents who choose to send their children to charter schools. I review the methods good schools use in creating a partnership between the school and the parents, including activities and processes you should look for in any school you would choose for your children.

In chapter 8, I focus on how technology can be effectively incorporated into a curriculum.

Chapter 9 looks at three issues that often drive parents to consider the charter school option: safety, student discipline, and special needs. If you are considering a charter school because you are dissatisfied with the safety of your local school, with the expulsion and suspension policies of your local school, or with the special education service provided by your local school, take some extra time with this chapter.

In chapter 10, I explain the importance of certain details. As exciting as the charter school option might seem, if the school is inconvenient, it may not be a solution for you and your family. This chapter reminds you to check out transportation and before- and after-school programs.

Chapter 11 looks at the process for gaining a charter to found a charter school and at some of the obstacles that can prevent a charter school from developing fully to reach its potential for its constituents.

Appendix I offers a range of interesting charter school facts, such as average enrollment and class size of charter schools, as well as the number of charter schools across the United States.

Appendix II provides additional resources, including listings of the state-level charter granting agencies, informational Web sites, and articles and books about charter schools and the charter school movement.

In appendix III, I conclude with a directory of selected charter schools, consisting of names and addresses. I also provide a list of schools approved to open in the future.

Although the charter school picture will continue to evolve, I have attempted, with the fine writing and editorial assistance of Janet Tabin, to make this book as accurate and up-to-date as possible.

This book will serve as your guide through an exciting and challenge task. I invite you to begin your homework here and now.

1

What Is a
Charter School?

A S THE DIRECTOR of a charter school, I get this question
at least once a month: What *is* a charter school? Most
people have read or heard about charter schools, maybe in a
newspaper or magazine article or on television. The average
person, though, does not understand what distinguishes charter schools from other schools, or how they work. And so they
are left wondering: What is a charter school? A charter school
is, in fact, a public school, but a public school with a difference. Even more accurately, a charter school is a public school
with several special characteristics. To understand what a charter school is, though, we need to clarify what makes a public
school a public school. The basic answer is simple: taxpayers
supply most of the money needed to run the school. The same
is true of charter schools. Private schools, in contrast, run primarily on money that students' families pay as tuition, sometimes supplemented by donations from other sources.

The key differences between standard public schools and
charter public schools lie in organization, structure, and focus.

First, most public schools are organized geographically. A school has students from a particular town or section of a town. In most places, several schools of different levels—primary and secondary—in the same general area are grouped together as a school district. The individual school is governed by district decisions. The district, in turn, must follow state laws, national laws, and contracts between the district and employee groups. All too often, once they have met the district requirements, the laws, and the contracts governing them, public school administrators and teachers feel they have little flexibility left to meet the needs of individual children or to respond to parents' concerns.

And *that* is what makes charter schools different, or is at least one of the principal qualities that distinguishes them. Charter schools are organized under special laws that can actually free them from some laws and requirements. Charter schools also differ from standard public schools in that parents get a say in which public school their child attends. Generally, in regular public schools, if a child's family lives in the school's territory—sometimes called its "catchment area"—the child goes to that school, period. The primary choice the family has, if they have concerns about the assigned public school, is to place the child in private school and pay the cost.

At the same time, a child living in a public school's catchment area *must* be accommodated. Suppose a neighborhood school typically receives about sixty first-graders each fall. Suppose the school has three rooms and three teachers for those sixty first-grade scholars each year. If one fall, eighty first-grade students show up, the school cannot just turn twenty of them away. All eighty must be educated.

Charter schools depart from these rules. First, a charter school is never the family's only option. Second, the charter school may be allowed to draw students from a wider area, not just its geographical catchment zone. In some states, school catchment area, school district, town, county, and even state boundaries can all be ignored. And just as the family can choose to place a child in a charter school, parents may also choose to remove the child if they think it isn't meeting the child's needs. They can then return to the assigned public school or seek another alternative.

At the same time, the charter school is not required to accept every child who lives in a particular area or every child who wants to enroll. If it is organized to serve sixty first-grade pupils and eighty children want to enroll, the school can accept sixty and decline twenty. As long as the school chooses its students in a fair and nondiscriminatory way, the school may accept the number of students it wants. Where demand exceeds available space, students are generally chosen by lottery.

Essentially, then, charter schools are a cross between public and private schools. Like public schools, taxpayers fund them. Charter schools may not charge tuition. Like private schools, they have wide latitude as to how they spend the money.

Charter schools are regulated in other ways that protect students and staff. They must meet the same health and safety standards required of all schools. They must respect civil rights. And they must meet financial and performance requirements set by the state. Furthermore, a charter school's own charter sets out requirements the school must fulfill, in many cases high performance requirements. They are, however, legally free to make many of their own decisions about how to operate the school. Charter schools receive waivers from most state and local school regulations.

Currently, thirty-six of the fifty states in the United States have legal provisions allowing for charter schools. You will find details on the situation in your state in appendix I.

The School Choice Movement

CHARTER SCHOOLS ARE part of a broader trend in U.S. public education. Many Americans are dissatisfied with the performance of their public schools and are open to alternative approaches for educating children. A large percentage of the American public is interested in finding better ways to educate students who are falling through the cracks in our educational system. At the same time, over the past fifteen to twenty years, multiple studies have shown that schoolchildren in the United States lag behind their counterparts in many developed nations.

Many people have ideas about how to solve the problems of the traditional public school system. Most involve giving parents of school-age children more choice and greater influence over their children's schooling. Some propose home schooling or vouchers for use in paying tuition to private and parochial schools. More and more often, parents desperate to find a balanced and sound education for their children are considering magnet schools, private schools, and charter schools.

To many, charter schools represent a public education alternative to private school voucher proposals. Many educators, parents, and politicians are attracted to the charter school idea. They can embrace the idea enthusiastically because it protects public education as an institution while providing for fundamental reform and systemic restructuring (Watkins 1995).

The charter movement stimulates such optimistic phrases as "Catalyst for Innovation," "New Hope for Public Schools," "Rebels with a Cause," and "Latest Best Hope in U.S. Education." The real force behind the charter school movement then, is the general public, a public concerned about the deterioration of public education and determined that something must be done to educate students more effectively.

The charter school movement reflects a hope and belief that a carefully developed competition between existing public

©PhotoDisc

schools and new schools can stimulate real and vital improvement in education. Advocates hope that charter schools will provide both innovative models for schooling and incentives for educators and others to improve the current system of public education. Parents, community members, school boards, and others are looking to the charter movement to prod established public schools toward change and improvement as they serve as models and show how this can be done.

Advantages of Charter Schools

EACH CHARTER SCHOOL developer has a contract with the state that specifies how the school will operate and what the school must do to receive public funds for a five-year period of time. The contract holds the charter school accountable for improving students' performance and achieving the goals of the charter. These contracts are similar from state to state.

In some states, legislation has freed charter developers from most regulations that apply to public schools. Charter school teachers and staff are not union members. There are no tenured teachers in charter schools. Apart from the basic safety and hygiene laws, some states release charter schools from almost all other legal requirements. In other states, the charter laws are more restrictive.

The charter school movement is rapidly building a record of success. I am often asked why I think this is happening. It seems to me that this success arises not from a single factor but from a combination.

The reduction in bureaucratic requirements helps. Without these requirements, teachers and administrators can be more flexible and creative in meeting the challenges of education. They can experiment more. Closely related to that, because charter schools have fewer administrative levels and tend to be smaller operations, they can function better. When students, staff, and administrators all know one another, people find they are more likely to share the same goals, to understand each other's concerns better, and to work in greater harmony. Individuals see the possibility of making a difference and making things happen. They still have conflicts, but they also have more and easier opportunities to resolve the conflicts directly.

Equally important is the empowerment of parents. When parents know they have a choice, they become clearer in their expectations. They may become more demanding, but at the same time they support the school more and are more involved in it. Parental choice seems to be a key factor that enables charter schools to do what traditional public schools failed to do in the last twenty years. That parents can choose a school that better matches their children's needs may be the very thing that leads to greater academic success for the child.

I am certainly not alone in my opinions. One researcher states, "A charter school could provide educational options for students, parents, and teachers; . . . increase learning opportunities by offering a particular curriculum focus, subscribing to

©PhotoDisc

a specific educational philosophy, or utilizing innovative practices (e.g., multi-age classrooms, year-around schooling). . . .
These schools are also designed to draw on teachers' entrepre-
neurial spirit and to offer them new professional development
opportunities" (Bierlein & Mulholland 1993, 1).

Earlier I said that charter schools might be thought of as a
cross between public and private schools. However, there are
some major differences among public, private, parochial, and
charter schools. Many of these differences focus on money and
curriculum, as well as on the school's educational philosophy.
Student body composition varies as well: A private school has
greater control over who attends the school. Private schools
can decline to enroll students whom they believe they cannot
serve well and can expel students who become disruptive. In
contrast, neither regular public schools nor charter schools can
control the makeup or behavior of students to the same extent.

Some of the impetus in the choice of charter school move-
ments came from comparisons among standard public schooling and other school options. Let's take a closer look.

Public Schools

PUBLIC SCHOOLS ARE open to the public, provided students live in the district. States and school districts must be sure they have enough schools to serve their student population. The school district decides how many schools will operate in the district from grades K–12. The state and school district determine all things, such as curriculum, class size, and hiring of staff.

Funding for public schools comes from federal, state, and local taxes. In most cases, property taxes are the largest source of school funding. They are paid by property owners within the school district. In areas where the school-age population is small or property is valuable, or both, the funding for schools may be quite generous. In contrast, where population is dense or property values are low, or both, school funding can be meager. Many people see this as the key source of inequity in public schooling. State and federal support makes up some of the difference. Nevertheless, per-pupil funding may be as low as $4,000 in one district and as high as $15,000 in another. Clearly, some districts are far better able to afford excellent facilities and the salaries needed to attract bright, well-prepared teachers.

Public education in the United States has a long, complex history. In their early existence, at a time when the well-to-do hired private tutors or sent their children to private schools, public schools were intended to provide an education to the common people. Schools had as their mission not only information and skills, but also a set of values and morals widely accepted by American society. Town residents often started a school when they saw a need; they'd contribute to the teacher's salary. The development of public education included a strong grassroots element, which is still reflected in the diverse make-up of school districts across the country.

In 1837, then Massachusetts' Secretary of Education Horace Mann explained the wide and growing support for publicly funded education with these words: "No political structure, however artfully devised, can inherently guarantee the rights and liberties of citizens, for freedom can be secure only as knowledge is widely distributed among the populace. Hence, universal popular education is the only foundation on which republican government can securely rest."

Private Schools: Independent and Parochial

APPROXIMATELY 26,000 PRIVATE schools operate in the United States today. About one-third of these are Catholic parochial schools, and about one-fifth are independent and nonsectarian. The remaining schools are generally run by other religious groups. When parents are dissatisfied with public schooling, they may consider private schooling if they can afford the tuition. And when the public is dissatisfied with public education, they often look to see if the private schools seem to be doing any better.

Independent, nonsectarian schools are open to a select group of students, based on ability to pay, academic potential, or any other criterion the school or its founders deem appropriate. Some are day schools, and students live with their families; some are boarding schools that provide housing and meals as well as education; many offer both day and boarding options. Private, independent schools are committed to the students they enroll, but they are not responsible for educating children in a particular area. These independent schools are supported primarily by tuition and by philanthropic funds. Many private schools offer a rigorous academic curriculum that prepares students to gain acceptance to some of the most elite private colleges and universities.

In addition, they offer strong extracurricular programs in the areas of art, music, and a vast array of sports programs. Many private schools also offer strong programs in foreign languages such as French, Spanish, German, Chinese, and Japanese, to name a few. Many other private schools have more specific missions. Some specialize in educating children who have learning disabilities, behavior problems, social difficulties, or even legal problems. Others might accept students talented in the arts.

A private school is supported chiefly by nonpublic funds and controlled by a private board of trustees. It is relatively independent of state control; conditions and regulations vary from state to state, but in general it has considerable freedom to set its own standards and curriculum, admit and dismiss students, and hire and dismiss teachers, without state supervision or control. It is free, legally, to incorporate religious teaching in its curriculum and is freer from political pressures when exploring controversial topics in the classroom.

Sectarian or religiously based private schools are concerned with the general education of their students, but usually their mission involves advocating certain religious beliefs. Catholic parochial schools are the most common sectarian schools and represent the second major type of school system, after public schools, in the United States. More than four million children are enrolled in Catholic elementary schools. Although their primary mission is to educate Catholic children, the schools are often open to other children as well.

Funding for these schools comes from student tuition and from church contributions. Like nonsectarian schools, private boards generally govern the school. In this case, the board has a religious affiliation and is guided by the church hierarchy. These schools are also relatively free from legal interference in their curriculum, teaching methods, staffing practices, and other operations.

Common measures of a school's success include student performance on nationally standardized tests and admission of graduates to competitive and selective colleges. Many students from private, nonsectarian schools perform quite well on national standardized tests. The schools are also rather successful in placing their graduates in selective colleges. Similarly, parochial schools have tended to outperform many public school districts on these measures of student success.

In the case of nonsectarian schools, careful research suggests that these schools' positive outcomes may have more to do with the specifically selected student bodies than with any particular practice by the schools. Although the students surely receive excellent educations and outstanding school experiences, the high standards for admission to the school suggest that these youngsters would score well on standardized tests and be admitted to selective colleges under other circumstances as well.

Catholic schools appear to be more successful with disadvantaged children than public schools generally are. Researchers attribute this largely to the social capital provided by the Catholic religious community. In other words, the dedicated staff and the supportive, respectful parent community seem to account for the greater success of these schools.

Charter Schools

LET'S TURN OUR attention back to charter schools. Again, charter schools are like other public schools in that they are free. Like public schools and in contrast to private ones, they cannot pick-and-choose their students. They must accept students on a free and open basis of some kind. Nevertheless, unlike other public schools, a charter school is not required to accommodate larger numbers of students than the school is organized to provide for.

Thomas, Benjamin Banneker School, K–8, Cambridge, MA

Juan Evereteze is the kind of kid who makes his mom glow with pride. From the time he started school, he brought home awards for performance: a science fair prize here, an essay contest honor there.

The problem was that these awards never came from his school. Away from school, he did great, but at school, his teachers reported that he was distracted and was not progressing socially. When his mother, Christa, suggested that he might settle down and focus better if he was given work that challenged him, his teachers said they would give him more challenging work when he settled down and focused better on the work he was being given. Around and around it went.

Something else about the situation worried Christa: It seemed to her that Juan and a small group of other students of color were often being called down for misbehaving when these children insisted they were not at fault. In addition, his teachers seemed continually surprised by the intelligence Juan displayed. Christa was troubled by these patterns, which the school administration attributed to teacher inexperience.

Juan was in the third grade when his mother heard something interesting through her office grapevine: Some people in the area were setting up a new school. Something called

Like most private schools and unlike most public schools, charter schools are governed by their own boards. That board, along with the school administrator, decides how to spend the tax dollars the school receives. They can decide to use the money where it will get the greatest result, where it has the greatest impact on students. Generally that means spending dollars in ways that put most of the emphasis in the classroom.

A charter school receives funding to operate from the district and state where it's located. These funds are based on a

a charter school, it was the response of parents and community members who—like Christa—believed the students of color in the local public elementary schools were being underestimated and underchallenged.

When Juan started the fourth grade, he joined the pilot class at Benjamin Banneker Charter School. There he found himself in an environment of firm but fair discipline and high academic standards. As his mother had predicted all along, he blossomed.

At Banneker, the philosophy calls for the teaching of social values as well as academics. The approach is moderately structured. The director is gentle but firm. Parents are a big part of the scene at this school: They work in the school or volunteer in the building. After-hour computer seminars help parents keep up to date with their children's technology curriculum. Attentive administrators and staff listen when parents have concerns.

Juan now balances his role as president of the Honor Society with his position on the school basketball team. Christa credits Banneker with carrying her son to a whole level above expectation in social, physical, and academic development. Juan's performance goes far beyond rote learning; he impresses his parents with his clear, critical thinking and his ability to take a position and support his ideas. Hard to argue with a kid like that—or results like those.

particular per-pupil dollar amount, depending upon the school district. The school's board of trustees and school director usually decide curriculum, class size, salaries, and hiring teachers and staff.

In general, children do not have to live in the district to attend a charter school unless specified in the charter. Some charter schools give preference to students coming from the local school district; most, however, don't draw district lines in their charter application.

Most students enrolled in charter schools are admitted through a lottery system; names of interested students are chosen randomly to fill the charter school's available spaces. Students do not need to go through a selective application process or score well on tests for admission. Parents only need to apply to the school and wait for the child's name to be called through the lottery process.

Charter Versus Charter

JUST AS CHARTER schools differ from independent private schools, from religious schools, and from other public schools, they also differ from each other. As a parent considering charter school placement, you will want to be clear about how charter schools can differ. These differences include all the areas educators think of as philosophy of education—what content the school focuses on, the approach to teaching, and the approach to assessing student achievement—all topics we will explore later.

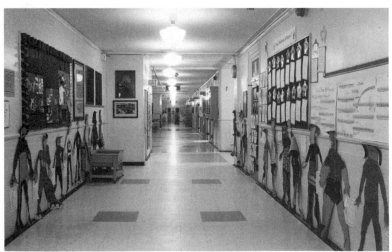

Management of Charter Schools

There is, though, another important way in which charter schools can differ from each other: how they are managed and by whom. Local community leaders, teachers, and parents started most of the existing charter schools. They did so because they had an idea for a school that they believed would better serve the children in a particular community. Most charter schools are designed to meet specific needs of students that are not being met by traditional public schools. In many cases, the organizers worked independently from any school district. In others they worked in cooperation with or under the guidance of a local school district. Both of these models continue to be used in the development of new charter schools.

In the past two years, however, several educational management companies have started charter schools. These companies are generally attempting to run schools on a for-profit basis, believing if they handle this responsibility correctly, they can make money for their investors. Educational management companies are not as likely to be as local as other charter school organizers, and so they would not know, in the same way, what the local children's needs might be. They are, however, likely to bring in start-up funding that does not come from taxpayers.

These, then, are the three broad categories of charter schools based on the nature of the start-up management.

1. A charter school created from scratch by teachers, parents, or community members with a particular approach to educating children.

2. A charter school created by the local school district. These schools operate independently and are exempted from certain district regulations, while still being a part of the local public school system.

3. A newly created, independent school run by a for-profit management company. This is the most

recent addition to the charter school landscape. A specific local charter school belongs to the company, which frequently has or plans to start schools in other locations as well. The management company usually has control over the kind of curriculum used and the hiring of teachers and staff. Later in this chapter I will describe the major companies that have entered this market.

The introduction of profit-making business organizations in the world of public schooling brings out a range of positive and negative reactions. Back in the early 1990s, when charter schools were opening in many states, those who founded these schools did it on a shoestring budget, with a great deal of effort and sweat from the community, parents, teachers, and staff. Now, we see a proliferation of private investors and companies who've decided that they can do a far better job of educating public school students and have determined that they can make a profit at the same time. During the past two years, the education-for-profit industry has mushroomed.

The theory and thinking behind this shift goes like this: If schools were run more like businesses, they would spend their resources more efficiently, resulting in more money allocated into the classroom and better accountability for student results. Advocates believe that students and parents should be viewed as customers to be served. If they don't like the service provided by one school, they can switch to another school of their choice that may be more sensitive to the needs of the customer. To gain and retain customers (students), the school must perform.

Along the same lines, advocates believe that the educational marketplace needs more competition before traditional public schools can change the way they educate children. The theory holds that competition will eventually eliminate bad schools, leaving only those that are truly meeting the needs of students and parents.

On the opposite side of the issue are educators who object to the very idea of turning public schooling into a market transaction. Some think this is risky business; to allow the business model in the school-house door could bring into question whether the bottom line for such companies will be the dollar or the education of its student population that it helps to manage. Many question whether in fact business has any business in education. Among those expressing caution is the National Education Association, which represents a large percentage of U.S. public school teachers.

Nevertheless, although the jury is still out on how successful for-profit charter schools will be, the door has been opened for any group who sees a link between business and education to try its hand at managing a school. At present, close to a dozen companies are managing for-profit charter schools. And for many who are deeply concerned about the education of children in public schools, especially inner city public schools, the need to improve education is so pressing that they are quite willing to consider this option. Most for-profit companies venture into education knowing full well that this is where the challenge truly is.

Most business start-ups are based on the theory of "find a need and fill it." In this case, the need is for better education in public schools, especially in urban and rural areas of this country. More and more of these companies are answering the challenge with the intent of doing a better job of educating those children who are missing out on the quality public education many students receive.

In mid-2000, a five-year contract was signed between the Inkster, Michigan, school board and the Edison Project, a for-profit school management company. The arrangement between the Inkster school board and Edison places Edison in charge of managing everything from the district's finances and staffing to curriculum development and instruction. This is

good news for education management companies, who see themselves as having the "right keys" to open the educational doors for more students and provide quality education in a public school arena.

Right now, for-profit schools are just a blip on the screen: they teach some 100,000 students at about 200 schools; the United States has 53 million children in school from kindergarten through twelfth grade. But if for-profit schools turn out to be a viable alternative, they could begin to give parents real school choice.

Deciding Which Management Style Is Right for You

Once again, choice brings responsibility. To determine the best choice, you must seek information, compare, think, and decide. In the case of for-profit schools, the choice depends more on what kind of education you think you need to provide for your children based on the particular needs of those children. If you are going to consider a for-profit charter school, the formula for determining the right school is the same one you would use to determine the right independent charter school, with a slight twist.

If you are considering a charter school under the management of a for-profit business, your investigation must include a review of the management company's ideas and approach. The educational philosophy and curriculum of an independent charter school is usually determined by people in the local school itself—meaning the school leader, board of trustees, teachers, parents, and community leaders. Many for-profit school management companies come with their own ideas on how the school should be run at the local level. The management company has the final say in school curriculum, hiring of teachers and staff, and the hiring of the school leader. Thus you must understand the management company's approach and the relationship between the for-profit management company and the local school's management.

The following provides a handy rundown on the theories and ideas presented by the major companies presently managing public school for a profit.

• *Advantage Schools.* Advantage Schools open and operate charter schools in urban neighborhoods where existing schools are failing to serve the students. Founded in 1996 and based in Boston, Advantage Schools "seek to create a new generation of world-class urban public schools."

• *Beacon Education Management, LLC.* Beacon Education Management is a K–12 education services company based in Nashville, Tennessee. Beacon offers a full range of contracted services to traditional public schools, charter schools, and private schools. The company was founded in 1992 and now provides education management services to schools in several states. The company oversees the overall operation of the school, including personnel, curriculum, and budget, under the oversight of the district or charter board. Beacon works with school communities to develop educational programs tailored to their needs.

- *Charter School Administration Services.* Charter School Administration Services (CSAS) is an education management company based in Southfield, Michigan. Founded in 1995, CSAS currently manages six charter schools in Michigan and one in Texas. CSAS has developed a "Charter School Planning, Development, Implementation, and Management Program" that is designed to guide charter school founders through the start-up challenges they may face.

- *Edison Project.* The Edison Project, founded in 1991, is a privately sponsored national effort to create innovative public schools that operate at current public spending levels and that provide all students, regardless of economic or social circumstances, with an academically excellent education. The curriculum places special emphasis on ensuring that all students master the fundamentals of reading and mathematics in the primary grades. At present, the Edison Project is managing more than seventy charter schools across the country.

- *Education Development Corporation.* Education Development Corporation (EDC), an education management company based in Grand Rapids, Michigan, was founded in 1995 specifically to open and operate public charter schools. EDC provides all the services necessary—including the site acquisition—to start and operate a charter school.

It currently operates eight charter schools serving more than 2,100 students in Michigan. EDC focuses on a "back-to-basics" academic program that stresses individual student involvement and direct teacher-student interaction. EDC schools stress extensive parental involvement in their children's education and are organized on the following seven principles (based on the Effective School Research): (1) safe and orderly environment; (2) clear school mission; (3) instructional leadership; (4) high expectations; (5) opportunity to learn and student time on task; (6) frequent monitoring of student progress; (7) strong home/school relations.

- *SABIS Educational Systems.* SABIS Educational Systems develops and operates primary and secondary college preparatory schools. Based in the Twin Cities metro area of Minnesota, it currently runs eighteen schools in eight different countries, including two charter schools in Massachusetts and two in Illinois. SABIS has broad academic goals, emphasizing a well-rounded education and based on a mastery of English, math, and a foreign language.
- *TesseracT Group.* The TesseracT Group, founded in 1986, is an educational management company with offices in Minneapolis, New Jersey, and Arizona. The company manages both private schools and public charter schools. TesseracT currently has contracts for twelve charter schools in Phoenix, Arizona. At TesseracT schools, teachers develop a Personal Education Plan (PEP) for each student. Using the PEPs as their template, teachers and students have daily review meetings and together set goals for student achievement. Parents also are involved in the development of their child's PEP and are encouraged to help students achieve the goals outlined in the plan.

In my opinion, it doesn't really matter who manages a school. What does matter is the education your child receives and the social environment he or she will be exposed to. If you are considering schools for your child, you need lots of information about schools in general and the schools available to you. Let's consider how you can evaluate a school.

2

Is This What Your Child Needs?

M ANY THINGS GO into making a particular school what
it is. They include everything from the building and
playgrounds to the director and staff, from the ages of students
to enrollment and class size, from the relationship with the
community to parents' commitment. But all of these elements
rest on a foundation: the school's mission and its philosophy.
So, as abstract as this might sound, you should begin your investigation of a school by looking at the school's foundation.

The missions of charter schools can vary greatly. The following examples of what could be charter schools' missions
make this point quickly:

To prepare students to pass the GED (high school
equivalence) exam

To provide an unstructured academic learning
environment

To serve the academic needs of gifted and talented students

To serve the academic needs of ethnic minority students

To serve the needs of "at-risk" students

©EyeWire

To provide intense math and science instruction to students

To serve the needs of students with learning disabilities
and special needs

As a parent, you must determine whether the mission of
the prospective school matches your child's needs and inclina-
tions. Sometimes this match is obvious. For example, a school
that prepares students age 16 and older to take the high school
equivalence exam is of no interest to you if your kids are middle school age.

But a mission that reflects a particular belief about how
children learn may take a little more investigation. It's not
enough to read and understand a charter school's mission. You
also must determine whether or not the school's mission
matches your own mission for your child academically. You
may have to learn something about educational philosophies
before you can decide, for example, whether an "unstructured"
learning environment is right for your child or children.

Further, you must find out about and understand the methods the school uses to accomplish its mission. Consider an example. Suppose a charter high school has a mission to graduate

most of its students. This mission might appeal to you and your children. For the school to accomplish its goal, however, students may be required to attend school two Saturdays a month and all summer. You may or may not want your child to spend every summer in school. If not, although the mission may appeal to you, the method may be unworkable.

Remember, a charter school's mission is more than a framed statement hanging on the classroom walls. Rather, it is the essence of what that school believes about children and their ability to meet these goals. It is not simply a feel-good statement; it is woven through every aspect of the school curriculum and environment. Everything a school does is centered on its mission, from the teachers it hires to the kinds of books it buys for the classroom. Teachers then can incorporate the mission into their goals for every student. When you observe the mission being used this way, you can be assured that the school is serious about the plan it has undertaken.

Charter School Mission Statements

ON THE FOLLOWING pages, you will find twenty-five actual mission statements from existing charter schools. Reading these should give you a much more solid understanding of what you can expect to learn from reading a mission statement.

Aurora Borealis Charter School
Soldotna, Alaska

MISSION: The purpose of Aurora Borealis Charter School is to provide the finest academic program possible, thereby increasing the opportunities for student success. It is our obligation to promote an educational environment that reflects high academic, character, and citizenship standards for all students and that establishes conditions where these standards can be met.

This is best achieved in a school where educational decisions are made by those who know the students best, the students' parents and their teachers.

EXCEL High School
Lake Havasu, Arizona

MISSION: Our mission is to provide educational services for youth of all ages without discrimination; to supply youth with the tools needed to be productive citizens and encourage students to EXCEL in all areas of life. To maintain an environment that allows those students who are "at risk" of dropping out of the educational process the opportunity to succeed.

Charter Community School and Extended Day Program
Placerville, California

MISSION: Our mission is to provide students with services ranging from daily to weekly classes and/or home study options. Students design individual study plans that range from 1 to 40 hours of instruction, weekly.

Core Knowledge Charter School
Parker, Colorado

MISSION: Core Knowledge Charter School's mission is to build a foundation of knowledge and skill that will enable our students to meet the challenges of a global society.

EXPLORATIONS Charter School
Winsted, Connecticut

MISSION: It is the mission of EXPLORATIONS to create a public high school that will cultivate a positive attitude toward life-long learning in an experimental, nontraditional educational setting. EXPLORATIONS will provide an environment that models interdependence as the foundation of society. It will emphasize activities that foster the acceptance of responsibility; develop positive decision-making and problem-solving skills; and encourage students to develop a healthier attitude toward their school, community, work, family, and, most importantly, themselves. Family and community involvement at EXPLORATIONS will demonstrate how each of us takes ownership in contributing to a better future for each other. It is the goal to develop students into adults who will be good citizens who value being productive role models in the community and see the need in "giving something back" to society. EXPLORATIONS is based on the motto: "Achieve Through Self-Discipline." Educational success is more attainable when the student is personally invested in the choices for their future.

Positive Outcomes Charter School
Dover, Delaware

MISSION: The mission of Positive Outcomes Charter School is to provide an academically focused education for students at risk of academic failure in a traditional classroom setting due to diagnosable psychiatric disabilities. . . . Students with Attention Deficit Disorders, Schizophrenia, Tourette Syndrome, and other disabilities, which contribute to their failure to achieve academically in a traditional class, will have the opportunity to complete their education in this school.

Dizzy Gillespie School of the Fine & Performing Arts
Stuart, Florida

MISSION: It is the mission of Dizzy Gillespie School of the Fine & Performing Arts to teach to ensure that all children achieve academic success. Professionally trained teachers and qualified staff, sensitive to each student, will teach music, dance, theatre, visual arts, and a balanced literacy reading program integrated throughout the curriculum in a fiscally sound environment.

Stone Mountain Charter School
Stone Mountain, Georgia

MISSION: The Stone Mountain Charter School's mission is to provide an integrated arts/academic curriculum that allows for individual learning, growth, development, and assessments in environments that promote freedom of movement, individualism, creativity, and safety for students. Using the Theory of

©EyeWire

Multiple Intelligences, this school design is based on learning and teaching in ways that address individual needs, talents, and interests. There is an ongoing School Development Plan based on the Comer School Design.

Innovations Public Charter School
Kailua-Kona, Hawaii

MISSION: The mission is that every student will experience learning successes; become literate, confident and caring; be able to think critically, solve problems, and communicate effectively; and become contributing and productive members of his or her community. Innovations' learning environment will be student-centered, foster the development and use of thinking skills, and allow students to learn by focusing on personally meaningful questions and engaging in related experiences that empower them as independent thinkers, decision makers, and problem solvers.

Francis Parker Charter School
Fort Devens, Massachusetts

MISSION: The Francis Parker Charter School's philosophy is based upon the nine principles of Ted Sizer's Coalition of Essential Schools and will address the needs of knowledge workers in the next century, preparing all children to use their minds well in whatever occupation they choose. Principally, this means developing intellectual skills in a few essential areas, such as writing, reading, mathematics, as they apply to rich "essential questions" that cross disciplinary lines rather than attempting to cover the content of many subject areas. As well as achieving a high level of competence in the core skills, students will work toward challenging goals in their individual areas of interest; the public demonstrations of their mastery will provide

©PhotoDisc

concrete and meaningful evidence in their readiness to graduate.

Michigan Institute for Construction Trades & Technology
Detroit, Michigan

MISSION: Our mission is to be a Super School. To provide timely, high quality, and cost-effective education and training to our students to satisfy building construction and technology demands. MICT&T offers students the opportunity to gain skills in construction trades & technology. MICT&T is a school-to-work program. MICT&T has developed relationships with employers. MICT&T guarantees employment to students who successfully complete our program.

Bluffview Montessori School
Winona, Minnesota

MISSION: The Bluffview Montessori School mission is to empower children to unfold all their potential as whole and unique persons in a world community. The school pursues this mission through distinctive Montessori approach, embodying individualized instruction, mixed age groups and international curriculum, a prepared environment, and Montessori teaching materials.

The Kansas City Foreign Language Charter School
Kansas City, Missouri

MISSION: The Kansas City Foreign Language Charter School is developing a French language total immersion public school for children in grades K–8. Its mission is to teach children to speak French with native proficiency and to prepare them for the best college preparatory high school education available.

Galloway Kindergarten Charter School
Smithville, New Jersey

MISSION: The mission of the school is to provide a full-day kindergarten program that balances both developmental and academic approaches to learning. We will use the Responsive Classroom techniques to instill caring and social responsibility in our students. We aim to create a lifelong love of learning, using active discovery methods and small class size (18 maximum). Teachers will be responsible for insuring that their students achieve minimum mastery levels and for developing individualized learning plans so that each child progresses at a rate appropriate for her or him.

Turquoise Trail Elementary School
Santa Fe, New Mexico

MISSION: The mission is to continue to creatively access and encourage the development of a curriculum centered around the interrelated theories of multiple intelligences and working styles to better meet the changing needs of its students in a rapidly changing world.

New Covenant Charter School/Urban League
Albany, New York

MISSION: The mission is to create a new generation of world-class urban public schools that will enable all children, regardless of socioeconomic background or prior academic performance, to reach the heights of academic achievement. Using proven instructional methods like Direct Instruction, teachers will educate students in the classical liberal tradition.

Lake Norman Charter School
Hunterville, North Carolina

MISSION: The Lake Norman Charter School will provide an alternative learning environment that provides:

1. a challenging academic environment
2. a focused classroom size (average of 20 students)
3. a strong discipline and honor code
4. a strong, cooperative environment for parents, students, teachers
5. high professional satisfaction and accountability

The Northwest Ohio Building Trades Academy
Rossford, Ohio

MISSION: The Northwest Ohio Building Trades Academy provides a pre-apprenticeship/school-to-work program of study for high school juniors and seniors interested in careers in the building and construction trades. Students follow a rigorous academic curriculum delivered through a post-secondary options program that allows them to earn college credit while they earn a high school diploma. In collaboration with local apprenticeship training programs, juniors participate in intensive career awareness and exploration activities that expose them to all the trades. Then they choose a field for a summer internship, followed by a senior year school-to-work experience where they alternate school and work weeks. Students are expected to meet 100% attendance requirement, wear uniforms and identification badges, and submit to drug testing before participating in work-based learning. This on-the-job work experience combined with rigorous academics will prepare students for entry-level careers in construction or admission to registered apprenticeship programs.

HomeSource-Bethel Family Technology & Resource Center
Eugene, Oregon

MISSION: The mission of the school is to serve Homeschool families with Technology & Resources. Technology, academic, and elective classes provided to homeschooled students and their families in a year-round program. Students may take between 1 and 15 hours of classes per week. Teacher-to-student ratio is 1 to 5 or one teacher and one aide to 10 students in most classes.

Sylvan Heights Science Charter School
Harrisburg, Pennsylvania

MISSION: The mission of the Sylvan Heights Science Charter School is to develop children who are equipped to meet the rapid changes of a high tech society through a broad-based interdisciplinary curriculum that highlights language arts, math, science, technology, and the arts. The mission will be accomplished through a partnership of family, school, and community in a culturally diverse environment that stresses positive problem solving, critical and analytical thinking, exploration and positive acceptance of differences between children, families, communities, and cultures.

Dallas Can! Academy Charter School
Dallas, Texas

MISSION: Dallas Can! Academy serves "at-risk" students in grades nine through twelve. This is a year-round charter school. The majority of the students has earned few or zero high school credits and read below grade level. The population is economically disadvantaged, basic skills-deficient youth who already dropped out of school or who are at risk of dropping out. Each student works on an individual learning plan. Most are in school half day and employed half day. The school day is divided between two hours of computer work and two hours of workbook/table work.

Tuacahn High School for the Performing Arts
Ivins, Utah

MISSION: The mission of Tuacahn High School for the Performing Arts is to enlighten minds, inspire talent, develop abilities, promote character, and preserve values, while training and encouraging students to meet the creative and intellectual challenges of the twenty-first century. Tuacahn High School provides an innovative and dynamic environment where all students are given the opportunity to succeed and excel in academics and the performing arts.

Blue Ridge Technical Academy
Roanoke, Virginia

MISSION: The mission of Blue Ridge Technical Academy is to provide "at-risk" youth in danger of failing the State Standards of Learning (SOLs) tests with entry-level technical skills required by local employers along with the academic preparation required to complete high school. We will also provide high school age students passing the State Standards Learning tests with entry-level technical skills required by local employers.

SEED Public Charter (Residential) School of Washington, D.C.
Washington, D.C.

MISSION: The SEED School provides youth with a nurturing environment and an exciting place to learn in a residential school environment. The SEED School is the first urban public boarding school in the District of Columbia, eventually serving 300 students in grades 7–12.

School of Technology & Arts (SOTA)
LaCrosse, Wisconsin

MISSION: SOTA is based on five constructs, namely: Nongraded, continuous progress classrooms; Assessment by performance, product and/or demonstrations . . . no letter grades; Customized educational programming option for parents; Arts and technology emphasis; Shared staff/parent school governance.

Beyond the school's mission is its philosophy. A mission statement defines the purpose of an organization. It often reflects something about how the organization intends to fulfill its purpose. But whether or not the mission statement gives any detail about methods, a school's philosophy will. A charter school's philosophy will tell you a great deal about the kind and quality of education your child will receive in the school.

When educators talk philosophy, they talk about curriculum, instruction, and assessment. A school's philosophy typically consists of a curricular model, an instructional model, and an assessment model. *Curriculum* refers to what students are taught, what information they are expected to learn, and what skills they must master. *Instruction* means the way that this material is taught. *Assessment* concerns how the school staff determines that it is succeeding, how it knows whether the students are learning what the school set out to teach them, and perhaps whether the school is meeting generally accepted educational standards.

In terms of curriculum, schools and educators tend to fall into one of two camps. One approach is called *holistic;* the other is often referred to as *core.* The holistic curriculum approach rests on a belief that learning must include a context and must give students a sense that the material is relevant before they can be motivated and willing to engage themselves in learning. A core approach focuses on conveying a specific body of knowledge based on the belief that there is such a "core" of information and skills that people must have to be truly educated.

Instructional models are commonly described as either student centered or teacher centered. Student-centered instruction rests on the belief that children come to school with a base of knowledge, and the teacher's task is to connect new knowledge with old knowledge so that the student is engaged in the learning process. A teacher-centered approach is more traditional. The teacher comes to a classroom possessing all the knowledge and information that a student will need to know and then conveys this knowledge to students.

Instructional models are also divided into direct instruction approaches and experiential approaches to learning. A typical example of direct instruction would be having a teacher demonstrate a specific procedure for solving a math problem and then having the students repeat the same procedure on a series of similar problems. To approach the same material experientially, the teacher would pose a situation with a problem to be solved; the problem would require students to use math. With guidance and support, the students are then expected and required to develop a process for solving the problem.

Finally, a school's assessment model is intended to help the school determine the strength of its curriculum, the effectiveness of its instruction, and, above all, whether students have learned the skills and knowledge that were taught. Assessment often, though not always, includes measurement to compare the school's performance relative to other schools. Assessment comes in many forms and serves many interrelated purposes.

Later we will return to each element of educational philosophy, examining them all in much more detail. For now, keep in mind that the very nature of the charter school movement is to encourage innovation. Nevertheless, many charter schools have intentionally chosen traditional goals, methods, or both. Others take full advantage of the opportunity to experiment as much as possible, hoping to find a method that meets the educational needs of all students.

Publishers of educational materials and other educators have incorporated some of the most popular philosophies into the programs they publish. These programs or systems of materials reflect specific educational philosophies. Sometimes schools, including some charter schools, buy these programs right off the shelf and use them without change. Many other charter schools use one of these learning programs as a base from which to create their own in-house programs. They take a packaged program and adjust it to meet the needs of their particular student population. You will probably find it very helpful to become familiar with some of these programs.

What follows are descriptions of five of the most popular educational packages used in public schools today. (This list has been taken from the program entitled "An Educators' Guide to Schoolwide Reform.")

Accelerated Schools

THE ACCELERATED SCHOOLS approach was developed in the belief that at-risk students should have the same rich curriculum and instruction typically reserved for the "gifted and talented." The approach's name signifies the developer's conviction that at-risk students must learn at an accelerated pace to catch up with more advantaged students. Thus the primary goal is for at-risk students to perform at grade level by the end of sixth grade. Under the approach, members of the school community are encouraged to work together to transform classrooms into environments where students think creatively, explore their interests, and achieve at high levels.

Central to this approach is the work of John Dewey, an educational philosopher who believed that an "effective education" in a democratic country implies faith in the potential of children and adults to understand and shape the world.

Research on the effectiveness of Accelerated Schools is limited. Five studies examined the effects of Accelerated Schools on student achievement. Four followed a single school for two years; the fifth compared eight Accelerated Schools with schools that had implemented other reform models. Of the two rigorous studies that report student effects, both suggest that the Accelerated Schools approach improves student achievement, at least on certain measures.

America's Choice

THE PRIMARY GOAL of America's Choice is to raise academic achievement by holding students to high standards in the core subjects of English, language arts, mathematics, and science. This includes proficiency in reading by the third grade, readiness for algebra by the eighth grade, the ability to write clearly and concisely by the tenth grade, and knowledge of biology, chemistry, and physics by graduation from high school.

The America's Choice School Design centers on five areas: standards and assessments, learning environments, community services and support, high performance management, and public and parent engagement.

As a schoolwide approach, America's Choice is relatively new, and rigorous research on student achievement outcomes is not yet available.

Basic Schools Network

THE BASIC SCHOOLS Network is organized around four priorities:

- Building a sense of community
- Developing a coherent curriculum
- Creating a climate that supports student learning
- Developing students' character

In line with these four priorities, the Basic Schools approach advances the following objectives. Students (1) are able to communicate effectively; (2) have acquired a core of knowledge; (3) are motivated learners; (4) feel a sense of well being; and (5) live responsibly.

Coalition of Essential Schools

THE KEY FEATURES of the Coalition of Essential Schools (CES) is the set of "Common Principles" that guide school reform:

- The school should focus on helping children learn to use their minds well.

- The school's goals should be simple: that each student master a limited number of essential skills and areas of knowledge.
- The school's goals should apply to all students.
- Teaching and learning should be personalized to the maximum feasible extent.
- The governing practical metaphor of the school should be student-as-worker, teacher-as-coach.
- The diploma should be awarded upon demonstration of mastery of the central skills and knowledge of the school's program.
- The tone of the school should stress nonanxious expectation, trust, and decency.
- The principal and teachers should perceive themselves as generalists first and specialists second.
- Teacher loads should be 80 or fewer pupils, and per-pupil cost should not exceed traditional school costs by more than 10 percent.
- The school should demonstrate nondiscriminatory and inclusive policies, practices, and pedagogies.

The CES is not a specific model of school reform. Rather, the Common Principles are to be used by schools to shape their own reform efforts—including curriculum and instruction—that fit their particular situations.

Co-NECT

CO-NECT IS a schoolwide approach that focuses on improving achievement by integrating technology into instruction, organizing lessons around interdisciplinary projects, and reorganizing schools into multigrade clusters of students and teachers. The Co-NECT organization reports that the approach is based on a large body of research on effective schools, primarily drawing from three research strands.

First, it draws from research showing that schools can improve student performance when the whole faculty focuses on achieving challenging, concrete, and measurable results. Second, it incorporates research linking increased student achievement with schools that allow teachers to take responsibility for a common group of students and promote close, sustained relationships among teachers, students, and families. Third, it encourages authentic pedagogy, which requires students to think, develop in-depth understanding, and apply academic learning to important, realistic problems. According to the organization, the approach also incorporates two other "best practices": using multiple standards of assessment and incorporating technology in ways that enhance student learning.

By their nature, charter schools vary; the decision makers at each school can use whatever educational philosophy they deem appropriate for their school and their mission. We examine philosophies, curriculum, instruction, and assessment in more depth in later chapters. First, let us turn our attention to the very practical question of how you, the parent in search of a school, might locate and investigate the choices open to you.

3

So You Might Want to Enroll Your Child?

"When parents who have exercised choice are asked to identify the characteristics that attracted them to their children's new schools, their responses usually focus on several factors: high academic standards; a safe, nurturing environment; opportunities for meaningful parental involvement. . . . The demand erupts from an on-the-ground understanding by parents that there is no future for children consigned to failing schools, parents who reject the unjust arrangement that limits choice to families that have the economic means to either acquire a private school education or live in communities where public schools provide a decent education. . . . Economically disadvantaged people, who historically have not been well served by either public education or the market, are not likely to be taken in by romanticized notions of one or the other. But they understand that both public schools and the market respond to clients who have the power to grant or withhold revenues needed for institutional survival."

—Joseph P. Viteritti, "School Choice:
Beyond the Numbers," *Education Week*

N ow that you have some idea of what charter schools are and why they seem to be succeeding where more traditional public schools have not, perhaps you are thinking about enrolling your child or children. Maybe you know of a charter school or two operating in your general area, or of an effort to start one. If you know of neither, you might flip to appendix III right now to see if the list shows any charter schools in your general area. If your interest is high, it is time to get serious about doing your homework.

To evaluate a school, you will need to talk to various people, read multiple documents, and attend some meetings and events. You are going to ask questions, listen, read, and observe.

Your first phone call should be to the school's director, principal, or head. Whether you speak directly to the school head or to a support person, ask to meet in person with the head at a mutually convenient time. You'll need at least half an hour.

Mention that you would also like to pick up copies of all the following items, if available:

The school's charter

The school's mission statement

Any other statements of purpose, philosophy, values, or beliefs the school is using to guide its operations

The school's curriculum guides

Recent annual reports

Recent state site visit reports

Schedules that show meetings of the board and school events

I promise you will understand what all of these items are by the end of this chapter.

Don't worry if the director's office staff suggests that you meet with someone other than the director or principal. The school might have a dean of students or someone else they will want you to meet first. In any case, your first meeting is not likely to be your last meeting—unless you come away from that meeting sure that the school is not the place for your child.

At your first meeting, your goals are

1. to get a sense of the director as an educator, as a leader and manager, and as a person (if this meeting is with the director);

2. to begin learning about the history and philosophy of the school;

3. to get all the reading material you can about the school;

4. to arrange meetings or contacts with as many of the following as possible: trustees, teachers, other school staff, parents of current students, and former students themselves; and

5. to schedule classroom observations.

Most charter schools have a waiting list of children who would like to enroll, especially at the primary grade levels (K–3). Therefore, if the school or schools you are looking into seem like reasonable possibilities, you may want to ask to have your children placed on the list immediately. You can always withdraw their names later if you decide that the school isn't for you.

I am sure you have noticed that I've already provided you with a lot of homework. Except for your early visit with the director or the director's chosen representative, you can do these tasks in just about any order. You can also stop at any point in the process if you become firmly convinced that you have made a decision about the school you are investigating.

Let's begin with that first, important meeting.

Meeting with the Director

THE DIRECTOR OR principal of a school is the school's educational leader. The leader sets the tone of the school for the teachers and staff. A leader who truly cares about kids and honestly views parents as a positive force in the school will

©EyeWire

attract like-minded teachers. Such a leader will inspire every-one in the organization, and his or her outlook and approach will be reflected throughout the organization. The leader has an inescapable effect on the teachers, students, and parents.

It's a fact that good leaders are not easy to find. Good school leaders are even harder to find. A recent *New York Times* article illustrates this point, starting with the headline "Principals Quit New York City at a Record Pace." The article goes on to state, "While other large cities across the country are also facing a shortage of principals, New York City is grappling with what experts say is the largest number of leaderless schools in its history" (September 30, 1999, pp. A1, B6).

It takes a special person to be a good school leader. This person must be able to meet many diverse demands—from teachers, school board members, the community, students, and, most of all, parents. In theory, any principal or school di-rector faces these demands, but those in regular public schools can get away with being less responsive and accountable. A charter school director, in contrast, must face the demands squarely. If that leader is not sensitive to parent and student needs, parents won't send their children to that school. This means that the charter school leader must be someone who likes people and is ultimately there to meet students' and parents' needs.

Most parents have known schools in which the school principal is inaccessible or too busy to see them. Many parents who've had children in traditional public schools have never had an opportunity to meet with the school's leader. In fact, you may have been surprised when I said a request for such a meeting should be your first step. But for parents considering sending their children to a charter school, such a meeting is perfectly normal, natural, and sensible. You are meeting with the person who is ultimately responsible for the education your child receives if you choose this school.

Accordingly, you must prepare yourself for the meeting by identifying the questions you want to ask the school leader directly. Five questions in particular will help you gain a solid sense of the person who leads the school and the school he or she is attempting to create.

Questions That Will Help You Learn What You Need to Know

First, does the school leader meet with parents daily, weekly, or monthly? Any good leader understands the need to communicate with constituents as often as possible. This is even more important for school leaders. The school's two most important constituents are the pupils and the parents. A good school leader spends as much time as possible in the classroom, so that daily, or at least weekly, the leader can assess the type and quality of learning taking place. In addition, a good school leader spends time with the children and tries to get to know as many as possible, not just those who are sent to his or her office by the teacher for disturbing the classroom.

Most important, a strong school leader builds a relationship with the school's main constituents, the parents. Because charter school parents have chosen to send their children to that particular school, the school leader has a responsibility to get to know every parent. By doing so, the head can determine what the parents' greatest needs are and respond accordingly. Parent-director meetings can take many forms: monthly parent meetings, parent morning coffee hour, parent lunchtime meeting, monthly parent night, and possibly a parent Saturday breakfast meeting. The head should also make time for individual parents who want to meet. If the school leader uses any combination of these, you'll find it a good indicator of how important that person thinks parental involvement is.

Second, how often does the school have open houses? A willingness to hold several open houses during the year is a sign of a strong leader, one who is happy to have parents and community members see the school. Open houses help the community gauge the progress students are making at a particular school. They also provide an opportunity for parents and the community to express their satisfaction and their concerns about the school in person. Charter schools in particular should be open to this process; the more often they hold these

©EyeWire

events, the more often they receive the feedback they need to improve the school.

Third, what is the leader's educational background? The background of the school leader is important. A person in charge of running a school does not necessarily have to have a degree in education. However, anyone who's going to run any organization must have qualifications and background needed to deal competently with people and use resources productively.

Course work in educational theory and in organizational management will help an aspiring school director understand what it means to run an educational institution. Thus when you ask about the director's own education, you are looking for evidence of such course work or its equivalent in experience.

You can determine the qualifications of a school leader by requesting a copy of his or her resume.

Fourth, what's the leader's previous experience? How long has he or she been a school leader? What other professional positions has the person held? Learning about the leader's previous experience will help you gauge the leader's quality and suitability for the job. Normally, a school leader with at least two years of experience managing a school will have seen and been part of many different situations involving children's behavior. An experienced school leader will know what to put in place both academically and socially to create an atmosphere in which students will thrive. An experienced school leader will set policies that will make a safe and nurturing school environment.

Fifth, what is the leader's vision and strategic plan for the school? Most good leaders are visionaries. They envision a school that believes in high academic performance—performance that reflects the school's mission—for all students. They then devise a plan to reach that goal. Usually, the leader works with the board of trustees, teachers, and parents to devise the strategic academic plan. The plan provides guidance for the immediate future, generally the next three to five years.

Bhatti, Benjamin Banneker
Charter School, K–8, Cambridge, MA

"My kids love school. They have good friends, and they are doing well." Those are the words of Claudine Bhatti. She is talking about her nine-year-old son, Shahzad, and her eight-year-old daughter, Nadia. With both children starting fifth grade at Banneker Charter School, Claudine and her husband, Majed Bhatti, are convinced they have reached the right decision for their youngsters. But it took some trial and error before the Bhattis found what they were looking for.

Claudine and Majed had concerns about the entire public school situation in Cambridge. When Shahzad was nearing school age, they worried about the things they heard—about the ill manners permitted in public schools and about the low academic standards.

In addition, Shahzad was going to miss the cut-off birth date for starting school by just a matter of days. So the family pooled their resources and started their son in a private school.

This plan usually consists of academic standards that students are expected to meet, a plan to help students meet those expectations, and a way or ways to measure whether they have. A charter school with such a plan in place knows where it wants to take its students academically and how to get them there.

Ask the director about his or her philosophy and vision for the school and about the plans the school has developed to create that vision. The most important message you should listen for in your conversation with the school leader is how he or she believes students learn best and what methods of instruction the school uses to maximize all students' learning potential.

Shahzad and Nadia spent several years in private school before the Bhattis decided that simply avoiding the shortcomings of public schools was not enough for their kids. The private school where Shahzad and Nadia started their education was organized on an unstructured plan and was held to a very relaxed agenda. Because Claudine and Majed were uncomfortable with this approach to education, they decided to reconsider their initial decision.

They found the answer to their children's school needs in the charter school movement, specifically at the Benjamin Banneker Charter School. Banneker's educational philosophy matches the Bhattis' philosophy well. In addition to their academic lessons, the children learn responsibility and respect for one another. Claudine likes the school's no-nonsense approach. A relatively structured instructional plan for learning is reinforced by small class size and two teachers to a classroom. Regular homework helps the youngsters establish good work habits. Above all, a strong curriculum and a safe, secure environment create the kind of school this family values.

The leader's philosophy is the one that classroom teachers are most likely to follow.

Throughout your meeting with the director, you should be looking for certain evidence that this person is the kind of leader who can create the school that you want for your children. A good school requires a leader who is, above all, creative. Creativity must permeate every aspect of the school and the leadership, in and out of the building. A creative school leader can handle all of the problems that come her or his way calmly, appearing to resolve issues effortlessly. School leaders these days must deal with situations far less common than twenty-five to thirty years ago—single-parent households,

©PhotoDisc

latchkey kids, weakened family support, and the like. This requires that leaders be particularly firmly grounded in their
commitment to create an educational environment in which
everyone can thrive, both students and staff, in the face of
these new challenges.

A recent study at the University of Chicago and the
Consortium on Chicago School Research found certain common elements among principals of productive schools. They
found that these principals include staff, teachers, and parents
in decision making while helping them accomplish their goals.
They also focus on student learning. These principals articu-
late a vision for their schools and invite teachers and parents to
amplify and shape this vision. They also set high standards for
teachers. They understand a great deal about how children
learn, and they encourage teachers to take risks and try new
methods of teaching. They visit classrooms regularly, demon-
strating their conviction and taking the instructional pulse of
the school. Finally, principals of successful schools get things
done. Teachers have the books they need when classes start.
Principals find academic and social support services for stu-

dents in need; helping these students also reduces classroom disruptions.

Watch and listen for evidence of such effective leadership as you talk with the director and, later, as you talk with teachers, parents, and others associated with the charter school you are considering. If you find positive evidence of such leadership, you probably have found a school that can meet the educational and social needs of your children. Ultimately, a school is only as strong as its leader.

Meeting with Trustees, Teachers, and Other Staff Members

BECAUSE THE SCHOOL leader is very important in shaping a quality school, you will need to talk to other people to confirm your impression of that person and of the school's quality. You should talk to school trustees or board members, parents, teachers, and other staff members. As you talk to these people, ask about the school's history, mission and purpose, philosophy, and approach. Ask teachers about their best teaching experiences and their worst. Ask them what and how they teach. Ask teachers about the toughest teaching challenge they've faced and how they handled it. Chapter 5, which focuses on instruction and teaching, provides more ideas about what you can ask teachers to learn more about them.

Talking to Other Parents

ASK TO SPEAK to at least a dozen parents who've had children enrolled at the school for at least one year. Remember the questions you asked the leader about parent and community involvement? Use your conversations with parents to confirm what you heard. By talking with parents, you'll gain valuable

©EyeWire

insight into the school leader and how he or she runs the school. This certainly will be one indicator of whether the leadership style meets your needs or the needs of your child. Parents can also tell you about the teaching staff. Ask parents what they like *and* what they don't like about the school.

Observing Classrooms, Board Meetings, Parent Meetings, Open Houses, and Other Events

YOU NEED TO make your own observations, too. Most likely, at your first visit, you will be offered a tour of the school, the building, and the playground. Begin immediately to pay attention to what you see. Beyond the tours, schedule as many visits as you can to classes and school events. In addition to attending any event open to the public, as a prospective school parent you may also visit many events open only to parents.

Your most important observations will come from your classroom visits. If possible, schedule them so you can observe the teachers that your own children are most likely to have. Chapter 5 guides you on what to look for during your classroom observations.

Reviewing the Literature

AS A PARENT considering a school for your child, you'll find some written records helpful. The key ones are the school charter and mission statement, the school's most recent annual report, and the most recent site visit report. You will also want to check for any locally published news about the school. And as we will discuss later, you will want to look at the school's curriculum guides. If the school has other statements of beliefs, values, or practices, you will want to read them as well.

Three of your key documents may need some explanation. Let me tell you about the charter, the annual report, and the site visit report.

The Charter

The school's charter is the document that defines the school's purpose and its learning objectives for students. It's a public document that every charter school possesses. It must be given to every parent and community member requesting it. The charter explains the school's goals and expectations for its students and all others involved in the success of the school. By reading through the charter document, you should get a clear understanding of exactly what the school's founders' intentions were in starting the school.

This charter document becomes your checklist and guide as you look at each particular charter school. Because all charter schools are different, you can easily compare them with one another. In addition to asking about the charter, you should ask the school's director if the school has completed an annual report.

The Annual Report

The annual report is a document that the school puts together that describes what the school has accomplished during its past academic year. Embodied in the annual report are statistics on the school. These include student enrollment data, types of academic and social support services students are receiving from the school, ethnic breakdown of students, results of student standardized assessments, and accomplishments the school has made in the community. The report will also reflect the certification and experience of teachers, awards and recognition of teachers, the school's financial status, state and federal grants received, money donated to the school, and school visitations by elected officials, community leaders, and others. In addition, the document usually highlights accomplishments of students and staff.

The annual report will help you determine how well the school is fulfilling the mission set down in the charter. It is your window to the school, letting you see inside and make your own personal assessment on how the school will meet your child's needs. Charter schools are in a unique position of needing to document successes while identifying things to work on for the next year. Unlike other public schools, a charter school needs to evaluate continuously everything it does.

Through such constant self-evaluation, a charter school is able to measure itself to determine if the direction it's taking is helping or hindering the educational success of its students. If the school determines that its course is not the best one for its students, it can change and redirect to a program that's more academically and socially profitable for its students. Many schools have used their annual reports as tools for identifying shortcomings and planning for improvement.

Most state charter-granting agencies read and rely on annual reports before doing annual school inspections, traditionally called *site visits*. The report paints a picture of the school that enables the agencies to focus on certain areas when visiting the school.

The School Site Visit Report

As part of the state-level governing of public schools, many states require regular reviews of public districts and public schools. The review takes the form of an on-site evaluation, or site visit. The site visit is conducted by a team of people who write a report of their findings.

A charter school site visit usually lasts from three to five days. The site visit team consists of four or five people, including one parent from another charter school and one state charter-granting official who was part of the original team that granted the charter. The site visit team meets with representatives of all the people involved with the school: teachers, parents, students, school director, and board of trustees. They tend to ask many of the same questions with each group, although they tailor questions to the particular group being interviewed.

The site visit team does not necessarily expect perfection, but it does look for the relationships and processes that are likely to create excellent results over time. Their report will give you a sound indication of how the school is doing. It will reflect the strengths and successes of the school, but it will also help you see where the school needs to improve.

Questioning and listening, observing and reading—I have given you a lot to do. But as a parent, you surely recognize that few things are as important as the education of your child or children. The time and effort that you invest in evaluating possible schools for your children will be well spent. Not only will you make the right decision, but also you will lay a foundation of knowledge and relationships with others at the school you ultimately select that will pay off handsomely for your children and yourself.

Now let us look more closely at the elements that make up a school's educational philosophy and operation.

4

What Are
They Teaching
the Kids?

I N H I S B O O K *Cultural Literacy* (1998), E. D. Hirsch Jr. writes about a letter he received from a parent concerned about the education her children were receiving. The mother of identical twins, she wrote to express her dismay that her children, who were in the same grade in the same school, were learning completely different things. How, she asked, could this be?

Hirsch notes that many parents would be surprised if they were to examine the curriculum of their child's elementary school. He implies that many school curricula do not contain the basic ingredients to provide students with a central core of knowledge, with information that is broad in scope and sequenced to build new knowledge on a foundation of existing knowledge. Hirsch urges parents to ask to see their children's school curriculum.

Similarly, I encourage you to do the same with any school your child attends and any school that you are considering. Ask for and read the curriculum guide. Does it specify the core content that each child at a particular grade level is expected to learn by the end of the year?

©PhotoDisc

When identical twins in two classrooms of the same school seem to be learning completely different material, a parent is entitled to know why. Unless the school can provide a clear explanation, this situation is a red flag.

Of course the same subject can be taught many ways, and this may explain the differences in the twins' classes. I am reminded of a mother who wondered why her neighbor's second grader was watching baby chicks hatch while her own second-grade daughter was observing caterpillars weaving themselves into cocoons. When she inquired, she learned that the second-grade science curriculum called for a unit on the cycle of life. The two teachers had chosen different demonstrations of the same principle. Even better, she discovered that at the end of the study units, the two teachers planned to bring the two classes together so the children could discuss what they had learned. Thus all the second graders would get to compare and contrast the cycle of life in insects and birds.

When curricula set clear expectations and teachers work together, learning opportunities multiply. But when teachers in a school do not know what children in other classrooms are learning on the same grade level, much less in earlier and later grades, they cannot reliably predict that children will be prepared with a shared core of knowledge and skills. The result of this curricular incoherence is that many schools fall far short of developing the full potential of our children.

A School's Curriculum

THE CURRICULUM IS the educational program. A school's curriculum defines a school's course of study, outlining lessons or classes that students are required to take to fulfill classroom, grade, promotion, or graduation requirements. A good curriculum sets standards that make sense and that all students can attain. The curriculum is the roadmap that the teacher follows in classroom instruction. A strong curriculum is clear, so students understand what they are going to learn. The standard by which you judge any curriculum is whether students are provided with a body of knowledge and information that enables them to connect new knowledge with old knowledge. Most school curricula consist of basic subjects and areas that will be covered over the course of the school year. Each grade's curriculum should build from what was covered the year before and should prepare the students for what they will be studying and doing the following year.

Since many charter schools are developed as innovative educational institutions, you may find some with nontraditional curricula. Whether you are looking at traditional or nontraditional schools, however, you still must look for certain things to determine how strong the curriculum is and what your child will be learning throughout the year. Beyond this, you should be able to see from the plan how your child will be prepared to go to the next level of education, whether the movement is from primary to middle school, from middle school to high school, or from high school to college. A sound curriculum is key to whether your child will receive a sound education at that particular school.

©PhotoDisc

One of the earliest writers on curriculum, Franklin Bob-
bitt, perceived curriculum as that series of things children needed to do and experience so they could develop the abilities to
participate in the affairs of adult life and to be all that adults
should be. Others have defined curriculum as a plan for learning.

All curricula include certain elements. A curriculum usually contains a statement of aims and specific objectives; it indicates some selection and organization of content. It may
either describe or imply certain patterns of learning and teaching, whether because the objectives demand them or because
the content organization requires them. Finally a curriculum
often includes a program for evaluation of the outcomes.

Principles for a Quality Education

ALTHOUGH WE UNDERSTAND by now that every charter
school has its own distinct mission, I believe there are some

basic principles that all charter schools must follow to guarantee each student a quality education. You should accept nothing less for your child. If a school seems to be skimping in the area of curriculum, you should seriously question the quality of education it offers to students. Every sound curriculum should have the following features:

- A sound curriculum must contain a statement of aims and objectives.
- A sound curriculum must have well-organized content (subject matter).
- A sound curriculum must manifest certain patterns of learning and teaching.
- A sound curriculum must show how it will evaluate what students have learned.

Each charter school has its own curriculum, usually developed by the school administration, the school's governing board, teachers, and parents, or combinations of all of the above.

Some charter schools decide to buy an off-the-shelf curriculum, designed by a commercial educational organization. Commercially prepared curriculums generally reflect a certain educational philosophy. In chapter 2, we looked at the underlying thinking behind some of the most popular commercial curricula. If a school you are considering is using one of these programs, you should make sure that the curriculum it chose meets the needs of the particular students it serves. You should make sure that the school's curriculum and philosophy are in line with your own educational philosophy.

Because most states have grade equivalent standards, any good charter school should be following the standards set forth by the state. Most states have specific grade expectations to which district schools must adhere. Most charter schools follow the same standards, with few modifications based on the population they serve.

Remember, although charter schools can be, and generally are, innovative in their educational philosophy and mission, there still must be a standard that they adhere to so that they educate students at and above the level expected of students outside of charter schools. In other words, charter schools must be innovative in ways that have positive impacts on student learning and educational outcomes. As a parent, you are responsible for ensuring that a charter school's educational philosophy and curriculum standards are in line with the state.

As the director of the Benjamin Banneker Charter School in Cambridge, Massachusetts, I try to assure parents in my school that their children will receive an education equal to and better than the best public school in Cambridge. I assure them by explaining our educational philosophy and our approach to learning. You should be able to approach any charter school director and ask for the same assurances.

Sample Curricula

ON THE FOLLOWING pages are the Reading and Writing and the Mathematics curricula for the Benjamin Banneker Charter School. You can use these as an example of what to expect from an elementary school curriculum.

Kindergarten

Reading and Writing

Students are taught print and phonemic awareness.

Students are taught the parts of a story and their functions.

Students are taught that print goes from left to right across the page and from top to bottom.

Given a spoken word, students are taught to produce another word that rhymes with the given word.

Students are taught to orally bend syllables into words.

Students are taught to orally blend isolated sounds into a spoken one-syllable word.

Students are taught to write the correct letters to represent a sound or sequence.

Students are taught to recognize common words by sight.

Students are taught to understand and follow oral directions.

Mathematics

Students are taught concepts of likeness and difference by sorting and classifying objects by size, shape, and color.

Students are taught to count forward from 1 to 31, from 1 to 10 by twos, by fives and tens to 50.

Students are taught to identify familiar instruments of measurement, such as ruler, scale, thermometer.

Students are taught to identify left and right hand.

Students are taught to identify top, bottom, and middle.

Students are taught to recognize shapes as same or different.

Students are taught to compare size of basic plane figures.

First Grade

Reading and Writing

Students are taught to read both aloud and silently.

Students are taught to read with fluency, accuracy, and comprehension.

Students are taught decoding skills to enable them to turn letters into speech sounds they represent.

Students are taught letter-sound knowledge to sound out unknown words when reading.

Students are taught how to predict what will happen next in stories and justify his/her predictions.

Students are taught to produce a variety of writings, brief stories, descriptions, and journal entries.

Students learn to use capitalization for the first word in a sentence, for names of people.

Mathematics

Students are taught concepts of likeness and difference by sorting and classifying objects.

Students are taught to recognize and write numbers 0–100.

Students are taught to count from 0–100 by ones, twos, fives, tens.

Students are taught to recognize the relative value of a penny, nickel, dime, quarter.

Students are taught to recognize dollars and cents signs.

Students are taught addition through using concrete objects and paper and pencil.

Students are taught subtraction through using concrete objects and paper and pencil.

Students are taught to solve basic one-step story and picture problems.

Students are taught to identify familiar instruments of measurement, weight, capacity, and time.

Students are taught to identify and draw basic plane figures: square, rectangle, triangle, and circle.

Second Grade

Reading and Writing

Students are taught to read aloud both orally and silently.

Students are taught to read with fluency and accuracy.

Students are taught to accurately decode phonetically regular two-syllable words.

Students are taught to use knowledge of letter sound patterns to sound out unfamiliar words.

Students are taught to accurately read single-syllable words and most two-syllable words.

Students are taught to reread sentences when he or she does not understand the text.

Students are taught to produce a variety of types of writing such as stories, reports, letters and poems.

Students are taught to produce written work with a beginning, middle, and ending.

Students are taught to use correct end punctuation: period, question mark, or exclamation point.

Mathematics

Students are taught number sense, to be able to recognize and write numbers to 1,000.

Students are taught to use a number line.

Students are taught to recognize fractions as part of a whole or set or region.

Students are taught to know addition facts to 18.

Students are taught to write addition problems horizontally and vertically.

Students are taught the inverse relation between addition and subtraction.

Students are taught to recognize the times sign (×).

Students are taught to solve basic word problems.

Third Grade

Reading and Writing

Students are taught to independently read and comprehend longer works of fiction and nonfiction.

Students are taught to orally summarize main points from fiction and nonfiction readings.

Students are taught how to pose plausible answers to how, why, and what-if questions.

Students are taught to produce a variety of types of writing such as stories, reports, poems, letters.

Students are taught to spell most words correctly and use a dictionary to check and correct spelling.

Students are taught to identify and use different sentence types.

Students are taught what prefixes and suffixes are and how they affect word meaning.

Students are taught to understand different types of poetry, both old and new.

Mathematics

Students are taught to read and write numbers in digits and words, up to six digits.

Students are taught to recognize place value up to hundred-thousands.

Students are taught to round to the nearest ten; to the nearest hundred.

Students are taught how to compare fractions with like denominators.

Students are taught to use mental computation strategies.

Students are taught basic multiplication facts to 10×10.

Students are taught to understand multiplication and division as opposite operations.

Students are taught basic division facts to 100 divided by 10.

Students are taught to make linear measurements in yards, feet, and inches.

Students are taught to compare weights of objects using a balance scale.

Students are taught to estimate and measure liquid capacity in cups, pints, quarts, gallons, liters.

Students are taught to measure and record temperatures in degrees in Fahrenheit and Celsius.

Fourth Grade

Reading and Writing

Students are taught to produce a variety of types of writing, including stories, reports, summaries.

Students are taught how to gather information from different sources.

Students are taught how to organize material in paragraphs and how to use topic sentences.

Students are taught how to use subject and verb in a sentence and how they must agree.

Students are taught what synonyms and antonyms are.

Mathematics

Students are taught how to read and write numbers up to nine digits.

Students are taught how to use place value up to hundred-millions.

Students are taught to use a number line and locate negative whole numbers on a number line.

Students are taught to recognize fractions to one-twelfth.

Students are taught to read and write decimals to the nearest thousandth.

Students are taught to solve problems involving making change in amounts up to $100.00.

Students are taught to solve division problems with remainders.

Students are taught to solve two-step word problems.

Students are taught linear measurement in yards, feet, and inches.

Students are taught to identify and draw points, segments, rays, lines.

Fifth Grade

Reading and Writing

Students are taught to produce a variety of types of writing, including reports, summaries, and letters.

Students are taught how to gather information from different sources: encyclopedias, magazines.

Students are taught to understand what a complete sentence is and identify subject and predicate.

Students are taught how to use correct punctuation and underlining or italics for titles of books.

Students are taught poetry, fiction, drama, myths, legends, and sayings and phrases.

Mathematics

Students are taught to read and write numbers in digits and words up to the billions.

Students are taught to recognize place value up to billions.

Students are taught to identify prime numbers less than 50.

Students are taught the greatest common factor of given numbers.

Students are taught the least common multiple of given numbers.

Students are taught to determine and express simple ratios.

Students are taught to recognize percent sign (%) and understand percents.

Students are taught to read, write, and order decimals to the nearest ten-thousandth.

Students are taught the commutative and associative properties.

Sixth Grade

Reading and Writing

Students are taught strategies for writing a persuasive essay, with attention to defining a thesis.

Students are taught how to write a research essay, with attention to asking open-ended questions.

Students are taught how to give a short speech to the class that is well organized and well supported.

Students are taught what a complete sentence is and how to identify independent and dependent clauses.

Mathematics

Students are taught to describe and construct simple right prisms, cylinders, cones, and shapes.

Students are taught to construct plane figures that exhibit symmetry about a line.

Students are taught to construct parallel lines and a transversal, using a compass and straight edge.

Students are taught to use the area formulas for these figures: parallelogram, triangle, circle, trapezoid.

Students learn basic algebra equations, mainly using numerical expressions.

Students are taught how to add, subtract, multiply, and divide mixed numbers and fractions.

Students are taught how to read and interpret statistical data presented in the form of tables and graphs.

Students are taught to translate statistical data into line graphs, bar graphs, histograms, and circle graphs.

Seventh Grade

Reading and Writing

Students are taught expository writing.

Students are taught to write nonfiction essays that describe, narrate, persuade, compare and contrast.

Students are taught to write essays with attention to open-ended questions.

Students are taught how to give a short speech to his or her class that is well organized and well supported.

Students are taught elements of poetry, fiction, nonfiction, and drama.

Mathematics

Students are taught three-dimensional objects, symmetry, angle pairs, triangles, and area.

Students are taught how to calculate surface areas and volumes of simple three-dimensional objects.

Students are taught to demonstrate by measurement both kinds of symmetry.

Students are taught how to construct a circle that circumscribes a triangle, using a compass and straight edge.

Students are taught how to use an area of a formula.

Students are taught how to work with whole numbers, fractions, and decimals.

Students are taught to understand algebraic equations and fractions and to solve problems and equations.

Students are taught to work with data, coordinated planes, proportions, geometric proportions.

Students are taught to read and interpret statistical data presented in the form of tables and graphs.

Students are taught to find a mean, median range, and mode in a set of data.

Eighth Grade

Reading and Writing

Students are taught expository writing and nonfiction essays and to narrate, persuade, compare and contrast.

Students are taught to participate civilly and productively in group discussions.

Students are taught to analyze and interpret literature for effects on listener.

Students are taught to use idioms, analogies, metaphors, and similes and to infer literal, figurative meanings.

Students are taught to evaluate structural elements of the plot, its development, and how conflicts are addressed.

Students are taught how literature reflects the heritage, traditions, attitudes, and beliefs of authors.

Students are taught to revise writing for word choice, appropriate organization, and point of view.

Students are taught to edit written manuscripts to demonstrate control of grammar.

Mathematics

Students are taught real number system as a coherent set of elements, operations, and properties.

Students are taught use of algebraic expressions, equations, and inequalities.

Students are taught linear and nonlinear equations, including direct and inverse variations.

Students are taught to represent equations and inequalities as graphs.

Students are taught to use graphs to solve problems and to illustrate, approximate, and verify solutions.

Beyond mathematics and language arts, elementary schools should cover science, technology, music, art, and physical education. If you would like to compare the educational philosophies and curricula of several schools, your local state charter school resource center can probably provide information on a number of schools. (Check appendix II for the address and phone number of your state's charter school administration.)

Broad-Stroke Versus In-Depth Educations

ONCE YOU DECIDE that a charter school has a strong curriculum, it's imperative that you find out how a school plans to impart this huge amount of information to students. Most institutions follow one of two schools of thought in how they cover these things. Some educators believe that students

©PhotoDisc

should be exposed to as many different academic subjects as possible, using a broad-stroke approach to provide students with some information about many subjects. Others believe in covering subjects in a very thorough manner, allowing students to explore a particular area deeply while not necessarily touching on all of the information in every subject. These two approaches have trade-offs.

If a school chooses to expose students to as many topics as possible, it ends up with students who are aware of many different subjects. Those students won't, however, know much about any one subject. In contrast, if a school opts to give students deep knowledge in some subjects, the students' broad, general knowledge will be limited.

For example, let's consider the study of English literature. Under the broad-spectrum approach, a student will probably learn the names and titles of key works for many major writers. A student who studied the subject under the depth-of-knowledge approach would be familiar with many or all of the works, the contribution, the style of work, and the biography for just a few major writers in the field. In the end, you must decide what you think your child should know.

Reviewing a Curriculum

TO BE A more knowledgeable parent, you would do well to read further on the topic of education and curriculum. One book I'd recommend to every parent is *Core Knowledge Sequence* (Core Knowledge Foundation, 1998) by E. D. Hirsch Jr. This book provides a detailed outline of content to be taught in language arts, history, geography, mathematics, science, and the fine arts. This core knowledge sequence is supposed to give all teachers of students K–12 a solid foundation on which to build instruction year by year.

You should consider the following six points as you investigate a school's curriculum.

• *How effective is the school's curriculum?* One true reflection of this is whether students are learning the basic skills they need to succeed at the next level academically and, above all, whether they are able to apply these skills in a practical way. Ask about the success of students who have completed the school's program. Wherever they are today, are they able to perform well? Don't hesitate to request names and phone numbers of graduates and to follow through by contacting them.

• *Is the curriculum based on research?* The leaders at every school should be able to explain to parents why they chose a particular curriculum for their school's students. A school's curriculum should be based on tried and tested research that shows how students can gain a level of mastery in a particular subject. Two curricula that have stood the test of research and have been used successfully in many schools are:

Success for All (SFA)

Core Knowledge (CK)

• *Is the quality of a school's curriculum consistent across grades?* Not only should a curriculum enable students to develop mastery in one particular subject, but ultimately it

SIX QUESTIONS TO ASK WHEN REVIEWING A CURRICULUM

- How effective is the school's curriculum?
- Is the curriculum based on research?
- Is the quality of a school's curriculum consistent across grades?
- Does the school's curriculum meet the needs of special-needs students? Is it adaptable?
- Is the school's curriculum well aligned with state standards?
- How involved are teachers in the design of the school's curriculum?

should also allow and require students to develop mastery in every subject on every grade level.

• *Does the school's curriculum meet the needs of special-needs students? Is it adaptable?* Any school that prides itself on having a strong curriculum should strive to meet the academic needs of all students. That students come to school with a variety of academic needs means that schools must be organized to meet them all. A solid curriculum is flexible enough that, with appropriate adaptation, it can meet the needs of handicapped, impaired, and learning-disabled students.

• *Is the school's curriculum well aligned with state standards?* More and more states are setting curriculum standards for schools to follow. These standards outline the kind and quality of information that every student should learn at every grade level and subject area. Any school you are considering should be one that aligns its own curriculum with the state's curriculum

©PhotoDisc

plan. This will be certification for you that the school sets high standards for its students to follow.

• *How involved are teachers in the design of the school's curriculum?* One thing that makes charter schools special is the level of involvement their teachers have in creating the school's curriculum. The more teachers are involved in this process, the more invested they will be in seeing that students learn the material.

Finally, remember that the strongest charter school is one with a sound, proven curriculum. It should teach the basics as well as solid content in each subject. Look for a curriculum that focuses on building students' skills while continually assessing whether they are learning these skills. The curriculum should be comprehensive, encompassing all of the basic subjects that every student should cover in a solid K–12 education.

The two most important areas to look at in any school's curriculum are language arts and mathematics. If these two content areas are not covered correctly, chances are that some students will have deficits that will prevent them from doing well academically in the future. In mathematics, methods of instruction can be particularly important (see chapter 5 for more information about instruction). Briefly, the best math instruction incorporates both drill-style practice and problem-solving activities to help students learn and master math concepts. In language arts, look for a balance of coverage encompassing reading, phonics, literature, spelling, grammar, penmanship, and composition or written expression.

All charter schools have one thing in common: high expectations for the success of all of their students. The mission statements of many charter schools proclaim that all students are capable of succeeding at their school. Unlike many traditional public schools, which tend to blame the students when they don't learn, charter schools look for solutions to problems that students may be having in school. Organizing a curriculum that is more compatible with student interests is one way charter schools attempt to motivate and serve their students.

Once you have determined that the charter school has a sound curriculum, you must then investigate its methods of instruction and procedures for assessing student progress. Let us, then, turn our attention to the options available for teaching students and for helping students learn.

5

How Are
They Teaching
the Kids?

ALTHOUGH YOU MUST ask what your children will be
taught, you will also want to know how they will be taught.
Five interrelated factors determine how teachers teach and how
students learn:

- The particular material to be taught and learned
- The theory of instruction or instructional ap-
  proaches used
- The teacher or teachers doing the teaching
- The students doing the learning
- The overall classroom and school environment

The value of good teaching and good teachers is hard to
overstate. Because teachers are so central to whether children
learn, we will look first at teachers, their impact, and a current
controversy about the way they are trained and certified. Next,
we will turn our attention to instructional theories and practices. Third, we will consider how class size and teacher motivation affect instruction. Finally, I will review and elaborate on
the process that I've suggested for looking into the instructional quality of a school.

©PhotoDisc

Many adults have had their lives irrevocably changed, for better or worse, by their teachers. Indeed, a student who has skilled teachers is more likely to succeed in school, and those with less-effective teachers may not do as well as they would with a good teacher. Internationally respected child development expert Rudolph Dreikurs believes that the fulfillment of a child's potential depends on whether the teacher perceives his or her possibilities and stimulates learning accordingly.

Most of us can look back on our lives and remember the teachers who really affected us. The teacher with the greatest positive impact was the one who knew how to engage us in the learning process. As a result, we became sufficiently interested in a particular subject so that we wanted to learn more about it. Good teachers know how to get students interested in the subject they are covering. The more interested students become, the more time they will spend trying to learn about a subject on their own.

Good teachers are facilitators who guide and enrich children's learning activities. At the same time, they must also be caring individuals who show concern for students, whom children trust as confidantes, role models, and mentors, and who can help students cope with adversity.

I firmly believe that, after parents, who are a child's first teachers and greatest influence, classroom teachers come next. Your child's teacher may spend more actual contact hours with your child during the school year than you do.

Loraine Monroe, writing for the *Boston Globe* in 1997, said it well: "No one can overstate a teacher's importance to a child's essential well-being. . . . When you are a superb teacher, you work from the heart. . . . Teaching is holy work."

In his book *Beyond the Classroom* (Simon & Schuster, 1997), Laurence Steinberg explains the importance of good teachers: "Students performed better when they had better-prepared and better-organized teachers. . . . Students score higher on tests of achievement when they have been taught by good teachers in good schools. . . . A good teacher can bring out the best in a student, while a bad teacher can squelch even the most motivated student's desire to learn."

Having recognized the importance of teachers, we are faced with the question of how you, as a parent, can identify good teachers and good teaching.

Teacher Certification

AS A SOCIETY, we place a great deal of confidence in official certification. We hope that by requiring people to get licenses or certificates attesting to their professional credentials, we can be sure that they are genuinely prepared to do the jobs they undertake. We want to believe that if a person is certified, in whatever field, he or she can provide good service to the public. I believe that teacher certification can be very valuable. Many people, however, have begun to question what it is that we are certifying with the present teacher certification system.

Most teacher certification programs are designed to certify teachers in either a subject area or a group of grade levels. Certification to teach at the lower grades usually involves study of child development and instructional theory. At the upper grades, teachers who want certification are more likely to need course work in a subject area. The common belief is that if teachers know their particular subject matter or are trained to teach at a particular grade level, then they are certified and qualified to teach.

Unfortunately, the system can produce certified teachers at the lower grades who understand how to teach but have gaps in their own knowledge of some subjects. Similarly, it can produce teachers certified to teach at the upper grades who know their subjects well, but who do not really understand how to teach the material effectively. The truth is that what we require teachers to do to gain certification may miss the mark in terms of what they really need in the classroom.

Teachers' Levels of Experience

Many teachers believe that what is taught in education schools is not what teachers need to know to be effective in the classroom. Most teachers report that the best way to become a competent teacher is to teach. Having young teachers learn on the job, however, is not an acceptable alternative if that means some students spend significant time under the guidance of underprepared or student teachers. Only programs of strong, supervised classroom practice, in which developing teachers work under highly qualified, experienced teachers, seem likely to produce acceptable results. As a society, we must find a way that guarantees that we will have people in the classroom who are capable of providing students with a quality education from the day they enter school.

Some believe that if a person really wants to teach, all he or she has to do is master a particular subject, and students will learn. Others believe that to be effective, a teacher must do more than know a lot about a subject. A person who wants to teach must also understand pedagogy, child development, and psychology, and must understand how to engage students in the learning process.

One thing is certain: A teacher who knows his or her subject is far better than one who doesn't. This is probably one of the most important elements of being a good teacher. A teacher can't teach what he or she doesn't know. Indeed, surveys have shown that one of the problems facing most public schools is that too many teachers are teaching outside of their major subject or the subject in which they are certified to teach.

Because so many people doubt the value of the current teacher certification requirements, charter schools generally do not have to hire only certified teachers. This means that even if you believe that certification guarantees quality teaching, a charter school may not offer that guarantee. But if you don't believe that certification guarantees quality teachers and teaching, what does? And how do you find out if the school you're looking at has effective teachers?

In chapter 3, I told you that you needed to schedule an appointment to talk to some of the school's teachers and some parents. Remember how I said that you are going to take time to observe some classes in session? Those are the conversations and observations that will give you the information you need—that, plus a little guidance on what you should look and listen for as you investigate. I am going to suggest topics to discuss with teachers and signs to look for in the classroom. But first we need to explore teaching methods just a bit.

Teaching Methods

AS WE BEGIN to consider what educators call theories of instruction, you will see how fascinating the process of learning really is. As you look at different ways of teaching, you will see that there is no *one* best way to teach. Rather, whether teaching is "good" depends on what material is being taught and to whom.

Consider, for example, how you learned to prepare a traditional family recipe or to do small household repairs. Chances are good that a parent or other family member taught you one-on-one or with a couple of your siblings or cousins. That kind of personal instruction is very effective and almost essential with some kinds of lessons. But you can probably also recall situations—maybe an exciting lesson in literature, history, or politics—when an excellent lecturer taught you very effectively along with a large group of other students.

With philosophies of education, educators tend to contrast student-centered instruction with teacher-centered instruction and direct instruction with experiential instruction. Techniques of instruction include lecture, demonstration, discussion, question-and-answer, drill-and-practice, group project work, individual seatwork (reading and pencil-and-paper tasks), and laboratory or workshop activities. Some of the expressions and phrases you may encounter include structured and unstructured approaches, "sage on the stage" versus "guide on the side,"

©PhotoDisc

and problem-based learning. You would need a short course to learn all there is to know about instructional techniques and theories. So, if an administrator or teacher uses an unfamiliar expression don't hesitate to ask for an explanation.

Closely related to instructional techniques are approaches to classroom management: the creation of an orderly, cooperative, and productive classroom atmosphere. In general, teachers who are skilled instructors have relatively few problems managing a classroom. Students who are productively engaged in learning are rarely disruptive.

A structured approach to teaching, when effective, results in an obviously orderly classroom. Direct Instruction is currently a popular structured teaching technique involving the use of scripted lessons. This method is based on the theory that students must be taught certain skills in a scripted fashion, in which every teacher in the school uses the same lesson plan for every subject. This approach ensures that all students will receive the same level and quality of instruction throughout the school and from grade to grade.

In contrast, an unstructured approach may result in a classroom that appears less orderly. Nevertheless, some students learn much more easily with unstructured approaches. An unstructured style of instruction allows a student to construct a learning plan that reflects his or her own rate of growth. This instructional model can come in many different forms, with various titles, but it's traditionally known as the Constructivist approach to learning.

An example of the kind of excellent teaching you are looking for is described in a report in the February 23, 2000, issue of *Teacher Magazine,* in an article by David Hoff. The teacher, Mr. Jackson, used solid instructional techniques, careful planning, and vivid, entertaining examples to engage students in the learning process. Most of all, he taught his students concepts that gave them the ability to solve problems and to think.

Waters, Paideia Academy, Grades 7–8, Kenosha, WI

When Jessica Waters moved from her Montessori primary school to the Paideia Academy middle school, it was a pretty natural transition. She went from a class of six children to one of about eighteen. Then she went from tiny Paideia to the public high school, where she became one of more than 700 freshmen. Her mother and father wondered if they had done her a disservice and not prepared her for such a situation.

Of course, there is an educational theory that says keeping children in small, nurturing surroundings through the preteen years is the very best way to prepare them for crowded, competitive environments later. Jessica's performance in high school lends some support to that theory: She finished her freshman year at the very top of her high school class. And she did not do that by becoming a grind or by isolating herself. She enjoyed her transition to high school, joining the girls' basketball and softball teams and singing in choir.

Paideia Academy, where Jessica completed the seventh and eighth grades, is part of the charter school movement. It is a school with a particular educational philosophy, known as the Paideia philosophy. Sharing some common heritage with the Great Books philosophy, Paideia instruction focuses

William Jackson begins class at 12:20 P.M. by posting a cartoon drawing of two rabbits on the chalkboard. Before he tells his eighth graders why that picture will help illustrate their current lesson, Jackson reminds them of the problem they solved the day before. If someone is paid one penny per day for a job and that wage doubles every day, then 20 days later, the person will be making more than $5,000 a day. That's the power of exponential growth, he says. Today, he tells his students that they will learn a different method of growth, known as the Fibonacci sequence. And the rate at which rabbits reproduce will play a significant role in understanding it.

on original writings and primary text materials. Students learn to engage in close reading and to develop and explain their ideas using specific supporting evidence from the text. Projects are often student generated and student lead, placing substantial responsibility on pupils for their own learning. Classes run on a seminar format, and the instructional approach is didactic and Socratic.

Lori Waters, Jessica's mother, first learned about the new middle-grade charter school from a small newspaper ad. Both Jack and Lori Waters were attracted by the Paideia philosophy, as they had been attracted by the Montessori philosophy for Jessica's early education. The timing could not have been better for them; Jessica joined the very first class at Paideia.

Jessica thrived at Paideia and clearly gained a great foundation for thriving in the future. The Waters are complete converts to the charter school idea: Lori Waters has partnered with an educator in their Wisconsin town to open another charter school, this one serving children in kindergarten through eighth grade and following the dimensions of learning philosophy.

Jackson, who has taught at School 2 for 16 years, has discovered a new way to impart knowledge. He and his fellow teachers have written mathematics curricula for the seventh and eighth grades that is a mix of New Jersey's academic standards and the Japanese curriculum. More important, they've changed the way they teach in an effort to help their mostly high-poverty, immigrant students understand the concepts of mathematics, not just how to operate formulas.

If a teacher knows his or her subject and is skilled in a variety of teaching methods, he or she *should* be a good teacher.

But two more issues can come into play, possibly defeating good instruction. These two issues concern class size and teacher motivation.

Class Size

The size of the class, or the number of students for which a teacher is responsible, influences the teacher's ability to use a full range of teaching techniques. Smaller class sizes—fewer than twenty students per class at the lower grades, for example—allow a teacher to be flexible in using all of his or her teaching skills. Larger class size tends to force teachers to use more structured and teacher-centered approaches.

A growing body of research shows that smaller class sizes do have a positive impact on student achievement. The abundant evidence convinces us how important school and class size are to a student's ability to learn. Traditional public schools have been assailed for their overcrowded schools and classrooms. These criticisms are valid; solid research supports the need for small schools and even smaller classes.

Certainly, large classes work well in some situations—orchestra and choral performance classes, for example. History and literature lecture sections at upper grades might be fine. But even in these cases, the large sections need to be balanced with smaller groups for closer instruction. Although some students will perform admirably whatever the class or school size, most work best in the environment of a smaller school and small classes. With smaller classes, teachers can give more individual attention to each student. In addition, small classes help students who are falling behind and need extra help. Academic achievement is not the only reason for smaller schools and classes. Mounting evidence suggests larger, more impersonal schools contribute to disturbing trends in student violence and other antisocial behavior. The research is irrefutable; small schools really do work. Charter schools do come in different

©PhotoDisc

shapes and sizes, so checking on enrollment and class size is one of your responsibilities.

Teacher Motivation

Finally, we want to consider teacher motivation. This, too, is an important factor in good instructional practice. In his book *A Letter to Teachers* (Jossey-Bass, 1991), Harvard University Graduate School of Education professor Vito Perrone explains how schools can undermine teacher motivation. "In too many schools, teachers are not expected to make significant decisions about what to teach. And the decisions that are open to them often have fairly rigid boundaries. Elaborate curriculum guides with detailed objectives organized around subject fields leave little room for the personal interests or inventions of teachers."

A recent survey done by the Pioneer Institute, a nonprofit charter school resource center in Boston, Massachusetts, examined why charter school teachers chose to teach at charter schools. Of those questioned, 51 percent named mission and

BASIC SIGNS OF A GOOD TEACHER

- Knows his or her subject matter.
- Has a clear understanding of how children learn.
- Teaches in a way that engages students in the learning process, using a variety of techniques and approaches.
- Designs lessons that reach all students.
- Can assess student progress.
- Assesses self.

philosophy as the reason for their decision; 47 percent opted for charter schools because they had more control over curriculum and instruction; 42 percent listed the quality of academic programs; and finally, 41 percent chose charter schools for the collaborative working environment.

Remember, charter school teachers decide to work in a specific school. This increases the likelihood that these teachers are happy and motivated and will therefore create a happier atmosphere in the classroom. This is important because the quality of teaching has a direct correlation with how much teachers like coming to work. High teacher motivation is one specific advantage that charter schools can usually claim.

You are ultimately responsible for ensuring that your child or children have good teachers and good teaching. I have emphasized the value of excellent teachers and explored various approaches to instruction. Now let's focus directly on the question of how you are going to judge the quality of teachers and instruction.

POSITIVE SIGNS TO WATCH FOR WHEN OBSERVING A CLASS IN SESSION

- The teacher is using strategies that maintain active student participation.

- Students are responding positively during interactions with the teacher.

- Students are on task a majority of the time.

- There is a cohesiveness and spirit of cooperation between students in the classroom.

- The teacher is using clear and organized direct instruction.

- The teacher has established classroom routines and clearly communicates classroom rules and procedures.

Evaluating Teachers and Instruction

TO LEARN WHAT you need to know, you are going to talk to teachers and parents. You are also going to observe several teachers in action in the classroom. Try to talk to as many parents as you can with children at various grade levels to get a balanced view. Include in your conversations and observations the teachers your children are likely to have in their first year at the school. If possible, sit in on classes in session at several grade levels.

What are you going to ask and what are you going to look for? First, when you talk to parents, ask about the teachers and the schools, about what they are happy with and what they are not happy with. When you talk to teachers, ask about their credentials, their previous experience, and their philosophies on education. What did they study? What have they done before?

QUESTIONS THAT WILL HELP YOU UNDERSTAND HOW WELL A TEACHER WORKS WITH PARENTS

- What can parents do at home to complement what is happening in the classroom?

- How can parents know on a daily basis what homework has been assigned?

- How does the teacher design the lesson to meet the needs of all students, whether they are gifted, average, or slower learners?

- What is the teacher's grading policy?

When you observe a teacher teaching, watch for indications of whether he or she has a clear command of the subject. Watch how the teacher employs techniques to engage and motivate students. Is he successful? Does she vary her methods? Finally, observe the quality of classroom management. If the classroom is in disarray and out of order, learning suffers. At the same time, order that generates tension and sacrifices a happy atmosphere is also a bad sign. If the room is orderly and the atmosphere is positive, learning is enhanced.

Keep in mind that if you and the school match, your visits are laying groundwork for future success. There is no better time to begin to get to know your children's possible future teachers. Let them know you, too. You are the only person who can provide teachers with the insight into your child that they need to meet your child's academic and social needs. Ask teachers about how they involve parents and the home in a child's education. A parent's role can vary, but you can only reinforce the things the teacher is teaching in the classroom if you are communicating with the teacher.

Finally, while you are in the school and in the classrooms, pay attention to class and enrollment size. Are you comfortable with what you see?

If you are happy with the curriculum and instruction, look next at how the school determines whether the children are truly learning the material and skills—assessment.

6

How Do They Know the Kids Are Learning?

"Children are tested in school so educators can make accurate judgments about children's knowledge, skills, or attitudes. Once the teacher makes a test-based interpretation about a student, then that interpretation can be used in a variety of ways. For example, the teacher can decide the child needs more instruction so that a particular skill can be mastered. Or, in contrast, the teacher might determine the child has already comprehended a certain set of information, so that it's time to move on to another topic. Then, too, test results are often used by teachers to help them assign grades to students."

—W. James Popham, *Testing! Testing!*
What Every Parent Should Know About School Tests

"Without good assessments, we cannot know whether effective learning has occurred."

—A. Oosterhof, *Developing and Using Classroom Assessments*

IN GENERAL, WHEN parents hear the word "assessment," they think "test." And whatever adults think, when kids hear the word "test," they think, "If I don't do this well, I'm in trouble." But assessment, well used, is much more than handing

©PhotoDisc

out papers and grading kids on the results. Assessment is the process of gathering information. Properly used, it guides good teachers toward better teaching and good schools toward better learning for all students.

It is true that assessment usually means having students perform in some way and evaluating the performance. Indeed, assessment is all about judgment and decision making. It should not, however, be about blame. Like a farmer appraising his crop at mid-season, a teacher assessing her students is looking to see what is going right and what she needs to change. Lisa Delpit, in her book *Other People's Children* (The New Press, 1995), drives the point home when she quotes a parent's question: "When the corn don't grow, we don't say what's wrong with the corn, we ask if it rained enough, if the soil was good, or if we planted at the right time. How come y'all always trying to figure what's wrong with our kids?"

In effective classrooms, teachers are continuously assessing their students. They assign projects; students turn in exercises; teachers evaluate lab reports. Teachers engage students in discussion, asking questions and listening for evidence of understanding or confusion. More formally, but still within the classroom, teachers regularly give written tests directly related to the material studied. If you talk to educators today about the results of schooling, you will hear such expressions as "authentic assessment," "portfolio assessment," "juried exhibitions," and "rubrics." Although the terms may be alien, their meaning is not. They reflect reactions to and concerns about the use of major, standardized tests. We are going to talk plenty about the subject of standardized tests, but first let's talk more about assessment that does not involve standardized tests.

Types of Assessment

TO EVALUATE WHETHER a student achieved the real goal or objective of a learning project, schools may use *authentic assessment.* How do we know if a child has learned to read well at his or her appropriate grade level? Easy enough: We can give the child something to read and either have her read out loud or ask her to read and then answer questions about what she read. If the objective of the lesson is for the child to understand how to count money and make change, how can we assess the outcome of the lesson? Have him demonstrate the process, either handling a real purchase or a simulated one.

Portfolio assessment simply means that children accumulate a body of work to reflect their progress. For example, if a class is learning to write persuasive essays, each child might build a portfolio of essays that shows increasing proficiency. Often children are encouraged to assess their own work, adding to and removing things from their portfolios to reflect their growing ability to do the task and to judge their own efforts.

A *juried exhibition* involves having students perform—write, speak, demonstrate, or whatever—with someone other than the teacher judging and evaluating their performances. The reason for this is simple. Assessing a student's performance also is an evaluation of a teacher's work. Even the best intentioned of us has difficulty judging our own efforts.

©EyeWire

A *rubric* is simply a checklist or guideline. Teachers or assessors may use a rubric to be consistent as they evaluate various student performances. Sometimes teachers give rubrics to students to help them shape their own performances effectively.

Educators talk about classroom-based assessment and authentic assessment to make the point that judgment and evaluation are continual; similarly, teachers adjust their teaching methods and instructional plans based on the results of evaluation. When you talk to the director and teachers at a charter school, you should be concerned if you *don't* hear them talking about on-going assessment.

In addition to these types of assessment, there are also the big, standardized national tests. These are forms of assessment that we cannot afford to overlook. Most charter schools use standardized tests to help measure students' achievement.

Standardized Achievement Tests

STANDARDIZED ACHIEVEMENT TESTS are supposed to measure a student's knowledge and skills, usually in a particular subject. Typically, students are tested in language arts, mathematics, science, and social studies. Some schools may also measure foreign languages.

In terms of standardized tests, charter schools are the same as all publicly funded schools. Many charter schools believe that their students need to take the same types of standardized tests as those used in the local school district. They do this to demonstrate that their students meet the same standards applied to other public school students. Charter schools can thus prove that their curricula and instruction equal or exceed those of neighboring public schools. Standardized tests are certainly one way charter schools can validate their performance.

As a parent interested in your child's educational progress, you may be interested in the different kinds of standardized tests as well as their purpose and value. As a parent choosing a school, you are probably well aware of the importance of viewing standardized test results of a particular school as an indicator of how good the instruction is. At the same time, if you believe that a school's standardized test results are the main indicator of the level and quality of instruction, you may be putting too much weight on one of many factors.

All schools need information based on broader, more standardized samples of performance than are provided by tests designed for use in one particular classroom. Schools need to measure educational growth from year to year, compare curricula or teaching methods, and measure integration of knowledge and transfer of skills. Schools also use standardized tests to place students in appropriate courses or programs.

Most traditional public schools use standardized tests as the principal ways of measuring student progress. Charter schools tend to use the same standardized tests as ways to measure

STANDARDIZED ACHIEVEMENT TESTS

- **California Achievement Tests**   Norm-referenced tests of knowledge and understanding in reading (vocabulary, comprehension), arithmetic (reasoning, fundamentals), and language (mechanics, spelling).

- **Comprehensive Tests of Basic Skills (CTBS)**   Norm-referenced tests that assess skill mastery in language and mathematics. The CTBS is comprehensive or balanced, covering reading (vocabulary, comprehension), language (mechanics, expression, spelling), arithmetic (computation, concepts, applications), and study skills (using references and graphic materials).

- **Iowa Tests of Basic Skills**   Norm-referenced tests that cover vocabulary, reading, comprehension, language skills, arithmetic skills, and work study skills.

- **Metropolitan Achievement Tests**   Criterion-referenced tests that measure skill mastery in reading (vocabulary, word analysis, comprehension), language (punctuation, capitalization, word usage, expression, spelling), arithmetic (computation, concepts, problem solving), and science (facts, concepts).

- **Stanford Achievement Tests**   Norm-referenced tests of academic progress (covers social studies, composition, science, reading, math, and literature).

student progress as well as to compare their students with those in the local school district. In addition to standardized tests, most charter schools use rubrics, portfolios, demonstrations, performance assessments, and juried exhibitions. To show student progress in a more comprehensive approach, charter schools balance all the measures against the results of the standardized tests. In addition, to assess schoolwide progress, many schools survey parents, track student behavior, and survey students.

Currently, there are five prominent standardized achievement tests widely used in U.S. public schools. Some states also use their own state-designed tests, requiring all public schools in the state to administer the test to all students at certain grade levels. The five prominent standardized achievement tests that the majority of states use are the *California Achievement Tests, Comprehensive Tests of Basic Skills, Iowa Tests of Basic Skills, Metropolitan Achievement Tests,* and *Stanford Achievement Tests.* (See the box titled Standardized Achievement Tests for more detailed information about each.)

Points of Reference in Standardized Tests

One of the appeals of standardized tests is that they allow a student or group of students to be compared with some established point of reference. On the face of it, this appears very useful. Many of these tests, however, have a problem. There are two different types of reference points—norm reference and criterion reference.

A norm-referenced standard compares students with one another. With norm-referenced measures, by definition, half of the students *must* fall below the midpoint or below average. Because we usually think of "below average" as not good enough, norm-based tests seem to assign half of the tested students to the "not good enough" category.

Criterion-referenced standards attempt to compare students with some objective measure of achievement rather than comparing kids with one another. With an appropriate criterion-referenced test, it is potentially possible for all students to meet the measure of success.

Most educators view criterion-referenced measures of performance as more desirable and useful than norm-referenced measures. Unfortunately, norm referencing is much easier to do than criterion referencing. Therefore, most widely used tests are standardized by norms rather than by criteria.

How Schools Use Standardized Tests

If the school you are considering is using a standardized test, you need to understand how a school uses it. You should ask the director what the school does with the test results. A quality charter school should use tests for placing students in particular math or reading groups, for planning or evaluating classroom instruction, and, in some cases, for identifying students with special academic needs.

More and more schools in the United States use standardized forms of assessment to determine how well they are doing. But there are also many who frown on the use of standardized tests as a way to measure the progress of students or to judge the quality of the education a school provides its students. The biggest concern is whether teachers end up teaching to the test rather than attending to the development of each child in their classrooms. In other words, too much of the classroom time and effort may focus on preparing children for taking standardized tests and teaching material the teacher knows will be on the test at the expense of other material.

Acknowledging that standardized tests overwhelm much of classroom practice, Harvard psychologist Sheldon White (1975) suggests that we are contending with "an affair in which magic, science, and myth are intermixed." Harvard educator Vito Perrone (1991) asks who actually believes that an individual's intelligence, achievement, potential, and competence can be represented adequately by any standardized test. He asks us to consider whether tests address the particular educational concerns of teachers, of young children, or of parents. Do the tests provide useful information about individuals? About a class? Do they help children learn? Do they provide essential information to children's parents? If you find yourself tempted to place a heavy emphasis on your child's standardized

©PhotoDisc

test scores or the standard test scores of a school you are considering, you, too, may want to ask yourself these questions.

Some people believe that effective schools can and should use standardized tests to guide the instructional process. In choosing the right charter school for your child, however, I would encourage you not to concentrate too much on whether a school has outstanding results on standardized tests. The scores do not necessarily indicate whether the school is a place where your child will learn or develop good academic skills. It's far more important for you to meet the teachers your children will have. Ask questions about the kinds of in-class and teacher-built assessments these teachers are using. Ask how a teacher uses these measurements along with standardized tests to better understand their students' strengths and weaknesses.

Ultimately, good schools and good teachers use tests to determine if the students are ready to go on to the next level of instruction or if the teacher needs to reteach the material to re-inforce it in the minds of some students.

According to a report issued by the U.S. Department of Education's National Study of Charter Schools for the year 2000, charter schools are held accountable for the achievement of their students. Some charter legislation speaks specifically of improving student achievement as a goal for charter schools. As stated earlier, nearly every charter school uses standardized assessments to measure student achievement, and most use other nonstandardized assessments as well. More than one-third of the charter schools use seven or more different types of assessments to measure students' achievement and gauge progress toward school goals (see table).

U.S. Charter School Study

Type of Assessment	Percentage of Schools
Standardized assessments	96.4%
Norm-referenced assessments	86.2%
Criterion-referenced assessments	62.1%
Student demonstrations of work	89.0%
Parent satisfaction surveys	82.5%
Student portfolios	81.4%
Performance assessments	73.5%
Behavioral indicators	75.6%
Student interviews or surveys	71.2%

As you investigate the charter school or schools you are considering for your children, here are some assessment issues to ask about:

- How does the school assess student learning? What methods are used?
- Is there a consistent approach across grade levels so progress can be tracked from year to year?
- Is student assessment used to help teachers change their practice?

7

Who's in Charge Here?

WITHOUT A DOUBT, the director and the teachers make a school run smoothly on a day-to-day and month-to-month basis. But the success of any school—any charter school certainly—depends also on three other groups. One of these groups is the board of trustees. Another is the group you are thinking of joining: the parents with children in the school. And the third is a state agency, an entity with the legal power to approve the establishment of charter schools and to determine whether existing charter schools are meeting the performance commitments they made to gain the right to open in the first place.

A school's board of trustees and the parents of a school's students have the power to make an adequate school better and a good school great. The state's governing authority has the ultimate power: It can close down a charter school that fails to deliver. Let's look more closely at boards, parents, and state accountability.

The Board

EVERY SCHOOL OPERATES under the guidance of a board, whether it is called a school board, board of directors, board of trustees, or something else. A board is a committee with certain legal powers. The number of members can vary, but in public education, they generally consist of five, seven, or nine people. The number of members on charter school boards differs, often consisting of seven to ten people, but at times having as many as twenty people. The board's size is significant; both large and small boards have advantages.

In large, urban school districts, the school board is responsible for governing many, many schools that serve thousands of students. For example, the board for the Chicago Public Schools is responsible for almost 600 schools and more than 430,000 students. In small districts, the board may oversee ten or twenty schools serving a few thousand students. A typical suburban district might have eleven schools with 4,000 kids. There are also small school districts, with one or two schools serving 300 to 600 children; though rare today, they were once numerous.

©PhotoDisc

Charter schools are more like those once-common small school districts. The board of trustees for a charter school governs that school and that school only. The board often consists of people with strong attachments to the school for which they are responsible. Some board members are likely to be parents or grandparents of the students. Others may be community members with knowledge or experience that is useful in operating a school. Lawyers, experts in education, and faculty members of colleges often serve on the boards of charter schools.

Whether we are talking about large public school districts, small districts, or charter schools, the governing board is technically responsible for everything from mission and policy to hiring and firing of classroom assistants. In large districts, clearly, the board must delegate most of these responsibilities. Seven people simply do not have the time to decide on all the detailed operations of all the schools in a large, urban district.

Not so in a charter school. The board is directly involved in setting school policies, hiring the principal or director, overseeing finance and budget, hiring and firing staff, and addressing various other issues of school operations. It is perfectly possible for every parent with a child in a charter school to know someone on the board well enough to pick up the phone and call that person at home if the need arises.

Ultimately, a charter school's board of trustees has the fiduciary responsibility for the school and is, therefore, legally responsible for all decisions made by the head of the school. The board usually must meet monthly, and all of its meetings are open to the public. Effective boards address important issues regularly and often. They engage in public debate, reflecting a clear recognition that they can't make good decisions for the school without weighing their choices. They listen thoughtfully to the recommendations of the school's head, teachers, and staff. They ask probing questions. They allow time for parents and other members of the public to comment on issues that come before them.

Taking the time to attend some of these meetings and see the board in action will give you great insight into the governing process in general and to any specific problems that a school may have. What you want to see at a board meeting is careful and thoughtful weighing of the issues. Ideally, all the board members should not think alike on every issue, but their differences should be based on substance, not personality or politics. Personality clashes or disagreements that seem to cause the same people grouping together on unrelated issues may signal trouble.

The Parents

BEING A PARENT yourself, you will probably agree when I say that parents play an extremely important and complex role in a school. It has almost become a cliché that parents today face many challenges unknown to earlier generations. Parents often look to schools to help them meet these new situations, and as a result, they are sometimes accused of trying to shift the burdens of parenthood onto schools. Fortunately, in my experience, most parents want help but have no intention of walking away from their responsibilities.

And in my ten years of experience with schools, children, and parents, I've realized one important fact about children's education: A school is only as good as the parents who support it. Even with the latest technology, a highly educated staff, a cutting edge curriculum, and a charismatic leader, parents still remain key. Without the full support of the parents, the students will not progress significantly in the long term.

One thing most educators and parents understand clearly is that the parent is the child's first teacher. A parent who is truly concerned about his or her child's education will support the school by reinforcing what is being taught. And a school—

QUESTIONS TO HELP DETERMINE BOARD EFFECTIVENESS

- How often does the school's governing board set and evaluate school policies?

- Is this governing board consistent in setting policies that enhance educational objectives?

- Is the school staff supportive of the governance?

- Are parents involved in the setting of new policies?

- Has the school board outlined a comprehensive school plan?

- Are roles among the governing body clearly defined?

- Is it clear who makes the ultimate decisions for school policies?

- Is the decision making a collaborative process?

- Are students and staff part of the decision-making process?

including the school director and staff—that sincerely cares about educating youngsters will offer parents many opportunities to support the school and the children's schoolwork.

Having sent two children through the public schools for twelve years, I know firsthand that some public schools are unwilling to involve parents in the educational process. In some cases, administrators and teachers seem to disdain parental participation, as if parents are necessary evils to be endured but not encouraged. One of the reasons so many parents want to pull their children out of public schools is the schools' unwillingness to welcome them as partners.

Hart, Paideia Academy, Grades 7–8, Kenosha, WI

When her daughter, Courtney, reached middle school age, Rebecca Hart was concerned. Courtney, a very good student, was quiet and somewhat shy. The Hart's live in a peaceful, almost rural area, but the public middle school in town has a big-city feel. Large and crowded, the school is hardly what one would call a nurturing and safe environment. Rebecca dreaded seeing what that school would do to her daughter.

Rebecca asked her daughter and her husband to consider an alternative: Paideia Academy, a charter school accepting about forty students at the seventh- and eighth-grade levels. Run by two longtime teachers with a demanding academic philosophy but a caring, personal feel for kids, the school looked much better to Rebecca than the regular public school. Her husband, Brian, had reservations. He wondered how a school that small could hope to match the program that a large public school could offer. Courtney wanted to stay with her elementary school friends.

But both father and daughter agreed to give Rebecca's idea a try. Courtney started seventh grade at Paideia, knowing

Here again, charter schools provide a sharp contrast. They are looking for ways to involve parents. Parents often serve on their boards. Some parents are employed by the school as teachers, teacher aides, secretaries, librarians, cafeteria aides, and so on. Even more parents volunteer, doing services that greatly stretch the school's budget. Charter schools recognize the benefit of having parents involved in the day-to-day operation of the school. Such parents better appreciate what it takes to educate a child and how large a responsibility it is to operate a school. Most charter schools also understand the necessity of involving parents as a way to spread the word about the school's success to other parents and the community.

she could leave at the end of the first semester if she still wanted to be in the regular middle school. But long before the semester ended, Courtney had lost all ideas of leaving Paideia Academy before her middle school graduation.

Brian and Rebecca knew that Courtney was happy at Paideia. They could see that she was studying and learning. But Courtney is their oldest child, so they found it difficult to know if she was learning as much as the typical middle schooler. It was only when she reached high school that they discovered what an academic edge Paideia had given their daughter.

The Harts certainly have no reservations now, as Courtney's younger sister, Whitney, reaches middle school age. Whitney will happily leave behind an elementary school where she was recently one of thirty-one students in her classroom to move to the small, nurturing, but academically demanding environment of Paideia. Brian and Rebecca are now totally committed, serving on the parent advisory counsel, coaching student athletics, and recruiting other families for Paideia. They are also investigating charter schools at the primarily level for their youngest child, Robert, who is still a few years away from middle school.

Nevertheless, as valuable as board service and work in the school is, nothing is more important to the success of a school and its pupils than the small, daily acts of support that you, as a parent, provide. These come in many forms: checking your child's daily homework, staying in close contact with the teacher, attending school open-house and parent nights, visiting your child's classroom once in awhile, and, finally, spending a few minutes reading with your child every night.

Few charter schools that I know of would turn away a parent who wants to become involved. As a matter of fact, most charter schools are parent-centered when it comes to providing a quality education for the children who attend the school.

© EyeWire

"Family involvement" is generally written into the school charter or mission statement. In some cases, parents are required to give at least one hour a month to the school. Many parents are very happy to commit to such a school requirement.

True parental involvement means a parent who helps to reinforce the skills that the school is teaching his or her child. One of the most important things a parent can do to help increase the child's academic skills is to read with the child every day. Research has shown that children who are good readers are more successful in school. In doing so, they become partners in their children's education; this kind of involvement encourages teachers and schools and enhances the quality of education that is going on in the schools.

When you are investigating a school, you want to confirm that the director and staff welcome involvement and support of parents. There are several ways to determine how important parent involvement is to a school. There are definite things that a school does that show the importance of parental involvement.

First, schools that are working to involve parents effectively provide a great deal of information in the form of individual reports, newsletters, handbooks, and schedules. Those schools hold open houses and assemblies to welcome parents. They use parent volunteers in the classrooms and libraries. And they survey parents and welcome input in other ways.

I repeat: Schools and school staff should never forget that parents are the child's first teachers, and continuing parent participation is paramount to the effective education of children. Look for a charter school that makes parents a part of the decision-making process in all aspects of your child's education. Look for a charter school that believes in parent involvement as part of the school culture, not as an afterthought. Once you find such a school, you will become an equal partner in helping to provide your child with a balanced education.

The State Chartering Agency

THE ONE THING that charter schools have over traditional public schools is their level of accountability. State agencies monitor charter school performance. If a charter school does

© PhotoDisc

INDICATORS THAT A SCHOOL WELCOMES PARENTAL INVOLVEMENT

- The school has a parent advisory council.
- A parent newsletter is distributed at least quarterly.
- Teachers send home weekly/monthly reminders of important events or assignments for parents.
- Parents receive a summary of the curriculum.
- Parents are provided a parent handbook.
- Parent surveys are sent out at least once a year.
- Parents are encouraged to attend monthly board meetings. The meeting schedule includes time for parent comments on issues.
- Parents are encouraged to attend at least two school open houses.
- Parents receive specific information on how to help their children learn.
- Parents are invited to offer suggestions on how the school can better meet their needs.
- Parents are recruited to serve on board-initiated committees to develop policies and address major school issues.

not meet the standards set, it may lose its charter. This accountability assures parents that the schools are doing what they set out to do in their mission statements. Some might say that charter schools are required to do things not demanded of traditional public schools. Many traditional public schools across the country cannot account for why so many of their students are failing to meet academic standards, yet these schools still continue to operate, without fear of being closed down and with much less concern that parents will pull out their children.

States vary in their levels of oversight, but every state that allows charter schools has a state agency, usually called a Charter-Granting Agency (CGA). This agency holds each charter school accountable for achieving the results set down in its charter request.

The CGA's role is to make sure charter schools live up to their promise of providing the kind of education they set out to, to every child who attends the school. In an article titled, "The Challenges of Oversight in a Deregulated System," Sandra Vergari highlights the roles CGAs play in monitoring charter schools. First, the agency is responsible for deciding whether to grant a charter to a group seeking one. If a charter is granted, the agency then monitors the school's performance and determines, based on how well the school is fulfilling its mission and goals, whether the school can continue to exist.

The title of this chapter asks *Who's in Charge Here?* I've examined the board of trustees, the parents, and the state agency that oversees charter schools. The board and the state agency are formed under provisions of law, and each has certain legal responsibilities. If they carry out their responsibilities successfully, the charter school you are considering is likely to fulfill its stated mission. But I also put parents in the category of people in charge. In the final analysis, it is parents who are and must be responsible for guiding their children toward success. Charter schools are designed to help parents do just that.

8

Technology

Is It Curriculum or Instruction?

TECHNOLOGY CAN BE used or misused in schools. When schools acquire computers or other forms of technology but make no coherent plan for its use, they often misuse it. Computers that are used simply as another mind-dulling drill-and-practice tool are worse than no computers at all. Fortunately, administrators and teachers in charter schools tend to know and understand how to use technology effectively in the classroom. Parents, too, however, should fully understand the best ways that schools can use technology so their children get the maximum benefit from it.

The simple presence—or absence—of computers does not tell a parent much about the quality of education in a school. In your search for the right school, you should thoroughly investigate how a school integrates technology into learning. Schools that use technology effectively are the ones that have a long-range plan for applying technology to increase learning, as well as for making real-world connections for students.

©PhotoDisc

An effective school technology program is based on a clear educational rationale. It would probably include a sequence of courses over several years. It would indicate not only what the children should learn to do with the equipment, but also how the equipment would be used to support and enhance other curricular objectives.

Correctly understood, computers, calculators, and most other forms of technology are tools, just as pencils, tablets, and books are tools. As using pencils and books—that is, writing and reading—are basic skills, so is using a keyboard. Today, knowing how to get on the Internet and find information on the World Wide Web is a basic skill. Like other basic skills, students are taught computer skills so that they can, in turn, actively use them for more complex learning. You would be concerned if you saw a school where children were taught to read in the first grade but then not expected to use reading regularly throughout the rest of their schooling. Likewise, a school that is preparing children to be full, effective participants in the world will teach them how to use technology—keyboarding, searching, and the like—and will then have the students use technology to support other learning.

Some educators do sincerely believe that the value of technology in classrooms and schools has been overemphasized. If you encounter that point of view, listen thoughtfully and ask the person to explain his rationale. He may have reasons that you will agree with and accept. Growing numbers of educators, however, believe that if students are truly going to be prepared to function in society, technology education must be mandatory for all students at all grade levels. In my experience, the majority of charter schools make technology an integral part of the curriculum and instruction.

A study by the state of Massachusetts concludes that technology can reduce the amount of time it takes to acquire certain types of knowledge by as much as 30 percent. Nationwide, teachers of all subjects are reporting increased student interest and motivation and higher quality student achievement when technology is used effectively.

Because of these reports, many schools have outlined the basic ingredients of a K–12 technology education for students. Most students should have a grasp of the following information before they graduate from any school, especially from a school that is serious about providing a strong education, like a charter school.

- Understand and have experienced the role technology plays in the practice of science, mathematics, and other disciplines.
- Be able to bring knowledge to bear on practical problems through the process of design, construction, and evaluation.
- Be able to collaborate, communicate, and work productively with others.

Students should be able to use the Internet and the World Wide Web for doing various kinds of research. Online resources should be used as another library at the child's disposal. Not only does the Internet offer access to many actual libraries, but it also provides many sites on topics of special interest. All major nations and many of the developing countries have Web sites—an unprecedented opportunity for students.

The information age requires different skills—skills that students did not need a generation ago. Today's students must know how to think critically, synthesize large amounts of information, and apply concepts learned from a global perspective. The Internet facilitates the achievement of many of the reform agendas that we have adopted in schools. Many wonderful, real-world examples illustrate the ways that teachers and schools use technology to engage kids and promote learning. Consider the following examples.

• *Student-centered education.* Smart schools will use technology to help provide more enrichment to students who need more one-to-one attention. Many computer programs are designed to help students improve their reading and math. Teachers can also use technology to monitor and assess students' progress over time.

• *Project-based learning.* Buying and selling stocks for the students is one example of project-based learning to which technology lends itself well. There are programs that allow students to participate in a virtual stock exchange on-line—essentially a computer game creates the experience of trading stocks. Schools that use technology in this way are the ones that know the value of technology as a form of real-time learning.

• *Integration of the curriculum.* Many charter schools believe that an integrated curriculum is one that allows students to learn more by connecting subjects such as mathematics and science. Technology provides short cuts to this process by allowing students to synthesize the two subjects by finding the things they have in common.

• *Work-based learning and technology.* Schools are also using technology to link the classroom to the work place.

©EyeWire

When they do this, students learn practical ways to use technology that will increase their future employment possibilities.

Here are some more excellent examples of how schools and teachers are using technology effectively.

• Students use CD ROMs related to subjects they're studying for research, along with books, maps, and other traditional print resources. Students also design Web sites with links to specific sites that contain more information on the given subject.

• A bilingual (Spanish/English) Web site, initiated by a group of parents, teachers, and community businesses and designed by students is a forum for student writing, program descriptions, and even curriculum links.

• Students use multimedia and database tools to maintain an archive of scientific information that they have collected from nature trails. They use the Internet to find answers to scientific questions and have developed an e-mail partnership with scientists from the area to help students with their investigations.

• At-risk and emerging readers view American Sign Language video stories, then use the computer to reconstruct the story. This process was developed to help students with reading, writing, and communication skills.

• Students are paired with adult volunteers from local businesses or universities to develop a joint research project on a topic related to science, literature, or social studies. They do the research using the Internet and publish the finished report on a home page on the World Wide Web.

These examples show just how innovative schools can be when integrating technology into the curriculum. Be cautious of a school that uses technology in place of teaching rather than as a supplement to better teaching. Let's face it: Technology is not the be-all and end-all of education. Nevertheless, students who attend a school where technology is fully integrated into the curriculum—taught and used—will be students who will have a leg up in higher education, as well as in the marketplace.

9

Think Twice About Safety, Discipline, and Special Needs

BARRING CONCERNS ABOUT educational quality, parents usually don't go looking for alternative schools when their children are happy and performing well in the local public school. But specific, nonacademic problems might set a parent off on a search for a different school. If your situation includes concerns about safety in the local school, the handling of your child's discipline, or provisions for special education, you will have particular questions you need to ask. Let's look at each of these considerations.

Safety

NEVER BEFORE HAS school safety been such an important topic. Shootings have occurred recently in a half dozen schools, both elementary and secondary. Many parents now send their children to school with a bit of trepidation, worried that they might get a call from the school telling them something terrible has happened to their child. In the past twenty years, some schools have turned into armed fortresses. They now have security systems in the form of security guards, closed-circuit cameras, and metal detectors.

Because most charter schools are small, they tend to offer a level of safety that many traditional public schools can no longer attain. Also, because many charter schools ask parents to volunteer to help in the school, the presence of many parents also reduces safety concerns.

Although the schools you're considering may be safer than other public schools, you should nevertheless ask to see the plan for emergency evacuation procedures. This plan outlines how the school safeguards students. Most schools put out parent handbooks and include these safety procedures there.

Discipline Policies

"CLASS DISRUPTION AFFECTS the teacher's allocation of time and attention, taking away teachers' autonomy to decide how to guide the class. Teachers often report having to devote a lot of time to one or two disruptive students, leaving little time for the others, who are usually being more cooperative" (Pritchard, 1998, Judd Publishing, p. 103).

Like it or not, suspensions and expulsions are facts of life in public schools. Removing disruptive students can be a matter of fairness to other students. Many parents send their children to charter schools because they are disgruntled with the way their previous traditional public school handled disciplinary issues, including the disciplining of their own children. One result of this is that a charter school may enroll some children with histories of misbehaving in school. The misbehavior

©PhotoDisc

does not necessarily stop just because the child is in a new school. And charter schools suffer the same ill effects from disruptive behavior that all schools suffer. Thus, in some charter schools, behavior problems can loom rather large.

As a charter school director, I have encountered parents who expect a charter school to be a lot more tolerant of students who cannot or will not follow the school's behavior policies. Some charter schools, in fact, *are* more tolerant. Some are designed with the mission of allowing students room to act out, with the hope that children will learn self-control through school incentive plans. Others, however, take a very no-nonsense approach to student behavior and conduct. Some allow even less misbehavior than traditional schools generally do. Some of these schools place heavy demands on students to adhere to strict codes of conduct. The results of these strict rules of behavior have been mixed. Some students do thrive in such strongly structured environments. But many students who already have difficulty following rules end up suffering in such a school environment. Some of these children need adults who can communicate and guide, rather than more rules. Additional rules and policies, such as "zero tolerance," fail to calm these children and often simply agitate them further.

Cotton, Bright Ideas School, K–12, Wichita Falls, TX

Claire Cotton was bored and apathetic in high school. A very bright student, Claire regarded school as a sentence to be endured. With almost no effort, she was making top grades and holding the third position in a class of 470 students. Despite a school life full of friends and activities, she felt she was treading water while waiting for college and for her real education to begin.

That was before Claire transferred to Bright Ideas, a charter high school in Wichita Falls, Texas. Six weeks before the end of her sophomore year of high school, Claire became ill. Her formerly excellent school performance started to drop steeply. Claire's parents were worried. Looking for a solution, they ended up solving more problems than they knew they had.

Claire had heard about Bright Ideas and its excellent academic standards. Becoming one of only eighty-five students in a school serving pre-kindergarten through high school graduation appealed to Claire; she was tired of feeling like a number. She knew this would be a new experience.

Charter schools are required to develop a set of guidelines that outline how students should behave within the school environment. Most schools have written policies and procedures that are voted on by the board of trustees that outline proper student behavior. The guidelines will likely explain students' rights and responsibilities. By providing to all parents such an outline of the behavior expected for students, a school displays a belief in fairness and due process.

The behavior policies of charter schools vary according to the schools' philosophies. As a parent, you need to become familiar with the suspension and expulsion policies of the school you are investigating. You may decide that the policies are either too rigid or too tolerant of student misbehavior. Knowing

Claire quickly discovered she was no longer expected to produce reams of busy work. As soon as she could demonstrate a clear understanding of a topic, she could move on. Freed from hours of pointless, repetitive tasks, she found that she was working harder and learning as never before. Sloppy attention to deadlines met with real consequences, and coasting was out of the question.

Claire discovered that Bright Ideas failed one of her expectations, however. Because she had heard about the high academic standards, she assumed all of the students were academically talented youngsters like herself. Just the contrary: Bright Ideas works with children of all intellectual capabilities, helping each child achieve his or her own personal best. Bright Ideas is a school where age does not rule; instead, children are placed where their individual needs can best be served.

At Bright Ideas Charter School, Claire Cotton discovered that learning can be challenging, even for the very bright, and that the right challenge makes learning a joy for every student.

your child's behavioral temperament, you must determine whether the school's environment is a good match, whether it is one that will help your child develop emotionally and academically. Your child may do well in one type of school environment and not so well in another. Making the effort to understand thoroughly the school discipline policies will help you make a wise choice and will increase the likelihood that your child will succeed.

Serving "Special Needs" Students

IF YOU ARE the parent of a "special needs" child, this section is important for you. You are the person primarily responsible for seeing that your child gets the help he or she needs in school. If you have a special needs child, you probably already know something about this subject. "Special needs" are numerous and variable. Some are easily identified and well established, as with impairments of sight or hearing. The legal requirements for serving children with these needs are fairly well defined. Other possible "special needs" are difficult to diagnose, less clearly defined, and controversial. These include various kinds of learning deficits, emotional problems, and gifted capacities.

Even with more clearly defined needs, the beliefs, theories, and practices for addressing needs are very much in flux just now, although they have certainly improved. In the early decades of the twentieth century, one state supreme court justified excluding a young boy with cerebral palsy because he "produces a depressing and nauseating effect upon teachers and school children" (*Beattie* v. *Board of Education,* 1919). Only thirty years ago in most states, even children with the mildest levels of disability were not allowed to attend school.

During the past twenty years, however, the education of children with disabilities has undergone a major change. The primary impetus for this change came from parents of children with disabilities and special needs, who demanded that their children receive the same education as those without disabilities. The federal government responded to this when Congress passed the Individuals with Disabilities Education Act, which mandated a "free and appropriate public education" for all children. Laws at the national and state levels now protect children who are classified as learning disabled or identified as special needs students. Parents of special education students need to know that the law is on their side.

Laws, however, are just laws. Meeting a child's needs still requires resources and trained staff. Like regular public schools, charter schools at times continue to struggle with methods and approaches for meeting the wide range of children's needs. In some cases, charter schools are still trying to determine what their responsibility is for providing services to special needs students. Every state governs charter schools differently, and state governing authorities vary in the requirements and exemptions they make for charter schools. Special education is an area of considerable variation and debate. Whether charter schools must adhere to special education rules the same way traditional public schools do is not always clear. Nationwide, charter schools have been grappling with the question of what they are required to do to meet the needs of their special needs students.

Many charter schools operate on shoestring budgets and lack the financial and administrative support of the districts behind them. Some charter schools have been accused of subtly discouraging parents of special needs children from enrolling their kids. Stories even circulate about charter schools refusing to serve students with special needs. Many charter schools do find themselves in a bind; they want to serve all the students who come through the doors but find the cost of serving an overabundance of special needs students a drain on the already tight school budget.

As a remedy, some of the best charter schools get creative about serving special needs kids. Some find that they can stretch resources by linking up with other area schools to share the services of counselors, occupational therapists, speech therapists, clinical psychologist, and so on. Other charter schools find imaginative ways of teaching all students without hiring extra support staff to meet the special needs of some. For some charter schools, serving the needs of particular special needs groups is their central mission. And some charter schools are experimenting with major innovations and departures from the current public school practices in serving special needs kids.

The Metro Deaf Charter School in St. Paul, Minnesota, is a good example of a charter school with a special education mission. The school enrolls only deaf students in grades K–6 and is nationally regarded as a model for the education of hearing-impaired pupils. American Sign Language is taught as the primary language and English as a second language.

Community Day Charter School in Lawrence, Massachusetts, is an example of a charter school experimenting with a significant departure from traditional methods of serving special needs kids. Community Day offers all of its students an "inclusive educational program" with no tracks and none of the individual education plans (IEPs) required and often so highly regarded in regular public schools. After pupil evaluations, parents are told their legal rights and then invited to waive conventional IEPs in favor of the school's ubiquitous "student services agreement." The school thus offers a unique education program to every child. Disabled youngsters are not labeled or made to feel different.

Since you know your child better than anyone else, you must be prepared to be his or her advocate. As a parent of a special needs student, you must find out whether a school has the ability to provide the specialized services your child needs. Although by law charter schools must provide the services indicated on your child's Individual Education Plan, you must determine that they have teachers and staff who are qualified and capable of working with your child. Ask to meet with the regular teachers and special education teachers who will be assigned to work with your child. Learn the school's philosophy on special needs students and whether it has curriculum and classroom instructional designs that will assist your child in his or her academic progress. Some instructional approaches for addressing particular special needs are much more effective than others. Thus you may need to pay special attention to the school's instructional philosophy.

SPECIAL QUESTIONS FOR THE PARENTS OF SPECIAL NEEDS CHILDREN

- How committed is the school to serving students with special needs?

- What kinds of schoolwide special education models does the school employ (inclusion, separate classes)?

- What are the qualifications of the school's special education teachers and coordinator?

- Are the school's regular classroom teachers provided with training to work with special needs students?

- Is the school's environment academically and socially nurturing for all students?

As a parent of a "special needs" child, you have an obligation to ask the kinds of questions that will reassure you and give you confidence that your child will be in a school that meets his or her needs academically and socially. Let's consider some questions you might ask.

How committed is the school to serving students with special needs? As I have pointed out, charter schools by their very nature are committed to meeting the needs of all students. Since the intent of many charter schools is to do things in as innovative a way as possible, these schools often find that it is not a problem to meet the challenge of providing appropriate academics for special needs students. Still, charter schools do vary in both their capacity to serve special needs students and their interest in doing so. I would suggest you avoid any charter school that seems to lack enthusiasm for the challenge of educating your special needs child.

Earlier I talked about Community Day in Lawrence, Massachusetts, a school using a very innovative approach with special needs kids. Community Day *is* enthusiastic about their program. But you may or may not be comfortable with a program that differs substantially from what your previous experiences have led you to expect. You may find such a program too far removed from what you feel your child needs. Although you may be attracted to a charter school for its innovation generally, you may find you have to choose between what your child needs and what the school is able to offer.

I have worked with parents of special needs children who were very attracted to a charter school, but ultimately did not enroll the children. As the parents came to understand the school's mission and methods, they determined that the approach was most likely not the best one for their child. Part of what makes the choice movement exciting is that it acknowledges that there is not one single right way to educate children, but there may be better and worse ways for any one particular child.

What kinds of schoolwide special education models does the school employ (inclusion, separate classes)? You as a parent need a thorough understanding of the model that the school uses in educating special needs students. Schools have many models to choose from, but two are most widely used. The first model is defined as an inclusion model; the second model is a separate classroom or pullout model. Of these two, more schools are using the inclusion model.

Many charter schools use this model for two reasons. First, parents of special needs children often prefer the inclusion model because they believe that keeping their children in regular classrooms better supports their children's social development. Second, it is less expensive.

The second model, the pullout model, is one in which individual students are pulled out of the classroom to get individual one-on-one attention. A certified special education teacher usually works with them. In some cases, a student might receive speech therapy, occupational therapy, or possibly a limited amount of behavioral counseling. Whatever services the school provides, you must thoroughly investigate whether such services will meet your child's special academic need.

What are the qualifications of the school's special education teachers and coordinator? A charter school's special education program is only as strong as the teachers and coordinator who run the program. When meeting with the special education department, ask what the qualifications of the special education coordinator are. A qualified coordinator should have a combination of five years of special education teaching and coordinating experience. Special education teachers should have at least one year of experience working with students with special needs. I stress the importance of qualifications because only qualified, experienced teachers and administrators will be able to design an individual academic plan that will meet the specific needs of your child.

Are the school's regular classroom teachers provided with training to work with special needs students? A school that is fully

©PhotoDisc

committed to meeting the needs of all its students will make sure that all teachers receive professional development training that will improve their skills in teaching these special student populations. Since most schools use the inclusion model, the school is responsible for making sure that all of its teaching staff understand basically how to design lessons that incorporate the varying learning styles of special needs students.

Since most charter school budgets allow for hiring a limited number of special education teachers, a school with an above-average number of students who have special requirements must devise ways of using regular education teachers to support this population.

Is the school's environment academically and socially nurturing for all students? As a parent, the bottom line in choosing the right charter school for your child is to find one that looks at the education of the whole child. Look for a school staff that believes that all children can learn and that all children are capable of developing skills that will make them life-long learners. A nurturing school environment is one where administrators, teachers, and staff are committed to ensuring that students feel that they are a part of a community of learners and are exposed to a rich academic environment.

Parents of special needs students commonly make two mistakes. One is withholding vital information from charter schools about their child's special needs. The other is expecting something from the charter school that they couldn't get the regular public schools to do. Many parents send their children to charter schools hoping for a magic all-in-one solution to their children's academic and social problems. These parents bear an additional burden as well—that of wanting their children to have no special labels attached to them.

If you are the parent of a special needs child, I encourage you to provide the charter school with all of the information about your child from the previous school. Meet with charter school teachers before school opens and inform them of the unique needs of your child. Sit down with them and help design an individualized academic plan that will get your child off on the right foot academically.

Finally, don't assume a charter school can do things for your child that a traditional public school was not able to do. This doesn't mean that you should expect nothing to change, but it does mean that solving your child's learning problems is rarely as simple as changing schools. To accomplish that, you will need to work closely with the school before and after you decide to enroll your child. Work with the school to achieve the outcome you want.

You can expect that a charter school, by its very design and purpose, will try as many innovative ways as possible to create a healthy learning environment for your child. Such an environment will foster your child's fullest intellectual and social development and will support his or her feelings of being valued and appreciated for the person he or she is.

In your search for the right charter school for your child, look more at the school's environment and atmosphere than at the facilities and services the school offers. Look for an environment that nurtures and respects all students regardless of their academic need.

10

Don't Forget the Details

Transportation and Before-
and After-School Programs

OR MANY PARENTS eager to enroll their children in a particular charter school, some details like transportation and open and closing hours seem incredibly trivial. They are willing to do whatever it takes to get their children to school. In that eager state of mind, it is easy to dismiss small issues as unimportant. However, transportation problems or lack of before- and after- school programming can create family stress and absenteeism. Stress, absenteeism, and tardiness can, in turn, undermine the family's very purpose for choosing a particular school. If a child cannot participate fully, that child may lose some of the potential benefit of enrolling in an excellent school.

Transportation

A WISE PARENT investigates what method a school uses to get students to and from school. Although sometimes either

Pitcher, Positive Outcomes School, Dover, DE

Commuting 100 miles a day just to get a youngster to school may seem like a lot to ask of parents. But for Dawn and Ben Pitcher, it was much better than the alternatives.

Dawn Pitcher had spent years helping her son, also named Ben, do every bit of his schoolwork at home each evening. When that wasn't enough to keep her distractible child on track, she sunk thousands of dollars into private tutoring to provide what her son's public school could not seem to provide. And even after all that, by the end of Ben's freshman year of high school, he was failing. What were the Pitchers to do?

The Delaware public schools where Ben Pitcher struggled never denied that he and his brother, Ryan, faced challenges that made the ordinary classroom environment incompatible with their learning styles. The schools simply had no ability to meet the needs of Ben and Ryan. Both boys accumulated perfect attendance records. Neither was disruptive; neither caused his teachers or classmates much trouble as they both slowly declined further and further.

The answer to the Pitchers needs came in the form of a charter school that specializes in the education of distractible students. Dawn Pitcher is quick to call Positive Outcomes School in Dover, Delaware, "our saving grace."

the school or the district might be required to provide transportation, this isn't always the case. A parent might be responsible for getting a child back and forth from school, whether by driving the child or paying for other transportation. I know of cases where a parent enrolled a child in a charter school but realized three-quarters into the school year that the family could no longer afford to send the child to the school because the cost of transportation was too great. As a parent planning to send your child to a particular school, you need to find out how your child will be transported to and from school and identify alternative means of transportation in case one way becomes too expensive.

Undoing problems developed in eight or nine years of inadequate schooling takes time. But the Pitchers were determined. When they first enrolled Ben at Positive Outcomes, one parent had to drive Ben twenty-five miles south from home to school and then return twenty-five miles plus another twenty-five miles north to go to work. At the end of the school day, the other parent repeated the process. The commuting continued for about two months until Ben reached driving age himself.

It took Ben most of his first year at Positive Outcomes to turn things around academically. But gradually, as he completed the ninth grade with some success, school became something Ben could enjoy. The tenth grade brought more improvement, and before too long, the Pitchers knew they had found what they needed. They enrolled their younger son, Ryan, to enter Positive Outcomes as an eighth grader the following year.

The mission of Positive Outcomes is to serve the needs of distractible students, generally youngsters with a diagnosis of Attention Deficit Hyperactivity Disorder. The typical class size is held to ten students or fewer. Teachers are selected for their knowledge, flexibility, and patience. And the results speak for themselves!

Transportation arrangements for charter schools vary from state to state. In some states, charter schools have certain transportation requirements that they must follow if they are going to receive dollars from the state or school district where they are located. A charter school may contract with the local school district or provide transportation service itself. In some states, the local public school district bears the responsibility for transporting charter school students. In other states, charter schools may or may not be required to transport students who are ineligible for transportation by a school district.

©PhotoDisc

Many charter schools can provide you with names of transportation companies who would like to transport your child and others to school. In addition, most states have transportation subsidies that enable parents to receive transportation vouchers for their child, based on income. And many states will reimburse parents for their own transportation expenses for getting their children to school if the parents take the time to fill out certain forms. Any school you are considering should know about these programs.

As an example of one state's approach, you may want to read the guidelines that New York State uses to coordinate public school districts and charter school transportation.

New York Charter School Transportation Regulations
• Within certain mileage limitations, a school district (except for a city school district) must provide transportation for

all of the children residing within its district to and from the school they legally attend, including charter schools.

• School districts may choose to provide transportation beyond the specified mileage limitations.

• School districts may use public or private carriers to transport children.

• Door-to-door transportation is not required.

• Charter schools are not required to provide any transportation for their students independent from that offered by their public school district to all public school children.

• A charter school may either contract with school districts to provide supplemental transportation or provide the transportation itself through the use of its own buses or public transportation.

• A charter school may want to set its own reasonable mileage limits beyond which it will not provide supplemental transportation to its students.

• Charter schools also may consider the practicalities of setting up and transporting from centralized pick-up points.

• Any charter school that opts to provide supplemental transportation through the use of its own buses must comply with a host of transportation safety laws, including requirements relating to equipment, inspections, and bus drivers.

Before- and After-School Programs

THESE DAYS, THE majority of parents need a before- and after-school plan for their children. With the surge in two-income households, as well as single-parent households, more and more parents are looking for safe places for their children to go after school. A tremendous body of research shows that a safe, secure after-school environment prevents children from involving themselves in delinquent activities. To be helpful to families, these programs must take into account the needs of

QUESTIONS TO HELP YOU EVALUATE BEFORE- AND AFTER-SCHOOL PROGRAMS

- What are the hours of the program?
- What kinds of activities are available? Is homework time provided? Supervised?
- What is the student-to-staff ratio?
- How many students are in the program?
- Are snacks provided in the program?
- Who is on the staff? What is the quality of the staff?
- What is the cost of the program?
- Are vouchers available?

both parents and children. A massive amount of federal legislation is being directed at communities, schools, and parents to help solve these problems.

Because charter schools are by definition innovative, most want to create more after-school programs. Charter schools by their very nature consider extended-day or after-school programs a significant part of their overall approach. These programs vary, depending on schools' resources and staffing. Within those limitations, charter schools decide what services they can offer to parents who want or need to place their children in after-school programs.

Most after-school programs run from 3:00 P.M. to 6:00 P.M. These hours usually accommodate the working hours of parents. Most after-school programs have a policy of charging parents a late fee any time a child has to stay beyond the program's closing time. Some schools have extended hours of school-type programming that go beyond the usual after-school hours. Most of

©PhotoDisc

these programs center on a specific course of study such as art, athletics, or music. Because these programs require teachers, not just simple supervision, they tend to be a bit more pricey than your usual after-school program.

You will want to know what kinds of activities are available in the after-school program. Some offer more activities and fewer academics. If you think your child needs more academic enrichment to bolster weak areas, you will want to know if academic help is available in the after-school program. If you feel your child needs more play and relaxation, you should consider that, too. I have found that most parents want their children to concentrate on their homework while they are in the after-school program. For many parents, having their children complete all of their homework during that time relieves both parents and children of the burden of having to deal with homework when they get home. Parents are generally relieved if they can go to work every day and send their children to school knowing that the school will be accountable for their children completing all of their homework. At the same time, when they do get home, parents and children have time to focus on tasks less related to school and to relax and play.

The best after-school programs are staffed by teachers or teaching assistants who work with the children during regular school hours. This way, students have the same adults working with them both during school hours and after school. The benefit of such an arrangement is that these adults know the children's needs and can offer them the same kind of attention they get during the day.

11

Maybe You'd Like to Start One of Your Own?

WE HAVE LOOKED at a great deal of information about charter schools and how to evaluate them. Maybe you have investigated one. And maybe rather than finding a school, you located other people like yourself who are interested in charter schools. Maybe you would like to know whether or not you and your group could start your own.

Or possibly you would just like to know what the existing ones had to do to get started. Let's look at the application process to gain state approval for starting and running a charter school. And let's look at some common problems that charter schools face in the process of getting started.

Each state that has passed charter school legislation has set up an agency to oversee the creation and running of charter schools and determine whether they are meeting the commitments outlined in their charter. (See appendix I for more information about states that have passed charter school legislation.) Those agencies, generally called charter granting agencies (CGAs), review applications from individuals or groups interested in starting charter schools. Based on their review, the agencies either grant or refuse the applicant or applicants a charter. The charter is a contract between the state and the applicant, giving the applicant the powers needed to start one of these special public schools and receive tax money to run the school.

Who Can Apply?

IN MOST STATES, teachers, parents, community residents, or groups made up of a combination of these can submit applications. Most often a group of people work together to make the application and, if successful, become the school founders. In some states, applications may be filed in conjunction with a college, university, museum, educational institution, community agency, state agency, or a profit-making or nonprofit business. In some states, existing private schools are not eligible to convert to a charter school; in other states, however, private schools can apply to become public charter schools. For a private school to convert to a public charter school, the private school cannot be affiliated with any religious group, and the board of trustees must be completely replaced with a new board. In some states, existing public schools may apply for charter school status.

A charter application includes a great deal of information. All the information and the plans reflected by that information must be consistent with the provisions and applicable laws and regulations of the state. In addition, all states require all charter school applicants to submit a full set of fingerprints to the charter-granting agency to complete state and federal criminal record checks.

In most states, a charter will only be approved if the proposed school meets the requirements as set forth by the state's

©EyeWire

chartering laws. The charter applicant group must be able to prove its ability to operate a school in a sound educational and fiscal manner. In addition, the group must make a persuasive case that its plans will improve student learning. In most states, charters are granted and renewed for terms of up to five years. Requests for renewal of a charter must be submitted to the chartering agency.

The Charter Application

CHARTER APPLICATIONS ARE very detailed. In most states, charter-granting agencies put charter applicants through a very rigorous process. Most states require applicants to be very specific when applying for a charter to ensure that the potential founders have the knowledge and resources to start and run a school.

The charter-granting agency must also ensure that the application process is open and fair and that all applicants understand clearly what the requirements are for competing for a charter. (See appendix I for more information about charter school legislation.) The next few pages outline the application process that most states use and the guidelines applicants must follow to be successful in being awarded a charter to run a school.

A typical charter school application asks for all of the following information.

Name of Charter School

Most charter schools use a school name that is synonymous with their mission. As you browse through the charter school directory in appendix III, you will notice names that reflect the school's curriculum or educational philosophy. Some applicants name their school after a person in history who exemplifies success and achievement. I doubt that the proposed name of the school much affects whether the applicant will be granted a charter to run a school. What it does do, however, is help give the school an identity, which is useful in attracting parents and students once the school begins operations.

Name and Occupation of Each Person in Founding Group

Since more than one person can apply for a charter, the background of each member of the group must be provided. I am certain that if an applicant group includes a person who is held in high esteem in academic and educational circles, he or she will lend credence to the application, and thus the likelihood that it will succeed increases. A good example of the value of a strong track record is reflected in this Boston story. Debbie Meyers became a noted educator by successfully running a school in East Harlem, New York. In her school, students showed tremendous progress academically for well over ten years. Ms. Meyers came to Boston and applied for permission to run a Pilot School. Her application was granted on the basis of her New York City record of success.

Name of Applicant's Partner

As I mentioned earlier, some charter school applicants invite partners to help them run a school. Partners could include a management company, state, city, community agency, and so on. Attracting partners means adding people who can provide additional resources and know-how. Such partners increase the likelihood that the school will succeed. Some charter school applicants partner with corporations who are interested in providing money, resources, and managerial knowledge to ensure that the applicant will be awarded the charter and ultimately run a school successfully.

These sorts of partnerships have opened up opportunities for profit-making educational management companies to come in with expertise in curriculum, instruction, personnel, finance, facilities, or sundry other help to increase the likelihood that an applicant will succeed. Most of these management companies have proven track records in running schools. I am sure this kind of arrangement has a positive effect on the likelihood of an applicant being awarded a charter.

Anticipated Opening Date of Charter School

Charter-granting agencies need to know when an applicant expects to open the school. In some states, once an applicant is given the green light to open up their school, they are granted a time by which the school must open. Many applicants delay their opening a year from the time they are awarded the charter so that they can prepare better.

Most charter school operators lack the necessary start-up funds needed to open the school immediately. They usually have to raise a certain amount of money to purchase books, desks,

Willis, Neighborhood House Charter School, K–8, Boston, MA

Meghan Willis was very pleased when Kevin Andrews wrote to tell her a new charter school was opening in her area. Meghan had placed her children's names in the Renaissance Charter School lottery, but their lottery numbers were very high, and enrollment seemed unlikely. Meghan and her husband, Larry Edelman, were considering private schools.

Meghan's oldest child, Mara Edelman, had finished pre-kindergarten, kindergarten, and first grade. Mara's little brother, Jake, was one year behind her. The class size at their local elementary school was approximately thirty children per section. Little Mara was worrying her first-grade teacher by doing second-grade work.

Meghan knew that Mara was not a child who created waves. Yet with a cooperative but bored daughter at grade one, both she and her husband wondered what would happen when less cooperative Jake outpaced his first-grade class. They grabbed the opportunity to enroll both children in the Neighborhood House Charter School in its very first year of operation.

Meghan Willis admits that the first year at Neighborhood House was a little rocky. The school faced many of the

school and administrative supplies, copier machines, fax machines, chairs, tables, and so on. One of the biggest hurdles facing most schools is finding a building that will meet the needs of their expected enrollment for the present and for the future.

Mission Statement

Charter-granting agencies look at the applicant's mission statement as a clear indicator of whether they will be able to operate a successful charter school. Most of all, charter-granting agencies can determine if the school's mission will both aid stu-

typical problems. Quickly finding and hiring a teaching staff involved some compromises. Every small decision had to be made, including when to start the school day. Working out an approach to discipline that was effective for children coming from many different backgrounds was also a challenge. The board, the director, the faculty, the staff, and the parents worked together to establish their appropriate roles. Meghan knew that new beginnings take special effort, so none of this surprised her. She credits the school's ultimate success to director Kevin Andrews. Right from the beginning, Andrews showed an admirable balance of personal judgment and openness toward parental input.

And a success it has been for the Edelman children. Meghan praises the school for knowing her kids, for working to challenge and enrich their educational experience, and for addressing issues directly when they arise. Mara recently gained acceptance to a selective admissions school, Boston Latin, where she expects to complete her secondary education. Jake, meanwhile, is happily wrapping up his elementary years at Neighborhood House. The youngest Edelman will enter Neighborhood House as a pre-kindergartener in the fall of 2001; he can hardly wait!

dents' academic success while enrolled at the school and prepare them for academic success in the future.

How Charter Will Improve Learning

The charter-granting agency places enormous importance on an applicant's ability to show how learning will be improved for students who attend the proposed school. This is probably the most important area outside of a charter applicant's mission statement. Since the whole intent of charter schools is to improve and enhance learning for their students, applicants need to demonstrate how they will do better than traditional public schools have done in the past.

Evidence of Community Support

Charter school applicants' abilities to show evidence of community support for their school will give credence to their claim that the school is needed and that the community will help them make the school successful. The success of a charter school is closely tied to its ability to garner support of its community.

Impact of Charter School on Nearby Public Schools

Applicants must show the impact they will have on neighboring public schools. The key reason for this relates to the tenets of the charter school movement—that charter schools will improve existing public schools through competition and through modeling better practices.

Proposed Board of Trustees

A charter applicant's board of trustees is an important piece of the puzzle determining whether an applicant will or will not be awarded a charter. The charter-granting agency looks to the board of trustees as having the fiduciary responsibility of running a school. In addition, the board of trustees is in charge of governance and setting policy for a school. Charter-granting agencies know that the stronger the board is, the stronger the school will be.

Director's Name and Background

The background of an applicant's director significantly affects the likelihood that a charter school will be successful. Many

©EyeWire

charter schools have problems in the first year because the leader lacks the necessary school experience. To succeed in that position, one must be able to lead a school staff toward the school's general success. A charter school leader sets the academic and social agenda for the school, ensuring that it will do well in both the short and long run. An applicant group that can prove that it has an experienced director lined up to run the school is likely to negotiate the application process successfully.

How the Charter School Will Promote Parental Involvement

An applicant's ability to show how parents will be involved in the school process also significantly affects the application's chances for approval. Charter-granting agencies are looking at this particular area because it seemingly sets charter schools apart from traditional public schools. The very intent of charter schools is increased parental involvement, offering parents an opportunity to become partners in the process of educating their children.

A charter applicant must show how parents will be involved in the day-to-day functioning of running the school, as well as in setting school policies.

Description of Admission Policies and Procedures

The proposed policies and procedures for admission to a charter school must meet requirements of state's regulations and laws. Most states require admission policies to be broad and unbiased in nature. In their admission policies, these schools may not discriminate against children on the basis of race, color, national origin, gender, disability, or on any other grounds disallowed for institutions that receive public funding. Charter school organizers must not propose using examinations or any other form of competition in selecting the students for the school.

The policies and procedures set forth in the school's handbook must be equitable in every way, giving any student the opportunity to apply to the school and an equal opportunity to be selected to enroll. All states are emphatic that any child who is eligible to attend public school is eligible to attend a charter school. Most states require that the schools accept all applicants, unless the applications exceed enrollment capacity.

To accommodate all applicants fairly, charter schools are required to create a lottery system that equalizes the chances for admission. Charter schools generally are allowed to give enrollment preference to children from a particular school district or city; thus charter applicants are allowed to write those preferences into their charter school applications. In fact, many people applying for charters give admission preference to students who reside in the school district where the charter school will be located.

Also, some charter schools write into the application process a preference for siblings who already have brothers or sisters enrolled in the school. Most states allow this, as long as the charter school applicant can show that there is a fair process for everyone who falls in this category.

Additional Information

Depending on the particular state, the application for a charter may also require answers to many of the following questions and requests:

- Where will the charter school be located?
- Will the facility be owned or leased?
- Describe transportation arrangements for students.
- Describe the building's physical facilities.
- Describe grade levels of students to be served.
- Describe the ages of the students to be served.
- What is the expected initial enrollment of the school?
- What will be the expected number of instructors?
- Describe the school's personnel policies.
- Describe hiring and firing policies.
- Describe student discipline policies.
- Describe student and staff dress code.
- Describe health and food services to be provided.
- Describe the overall school curriculum to be used.
- Describe the student population to be served.
- Describe requirements for graduation.
- Describe student achievement standards.
- Describe what standards of measurement will be used for students.
- Provide a detailed expected school budget.
- Provide a three-year financial plan.
- Provide start-up budget plans.
- Describe the insurance plan to be used by the school.
- Describe plans for physical expansion of the building.

©EyeWire

- Describe plans for a move to a new location for the future.
- Describe plans for student and school records transfer in the event that the charter is not renewed.

The requirements vary with each state's laws for charter schools. Contact your local state charter-granting agency to find out the requirements for charter applicants in your state.

Start-Up Struggles

FROM MONEY NEEDS to local opposition, from locating appropriate facilities to hiring quality staff, from conflicts among the organizers themselves to deadline struggles, charter school founders must address many problems.

A study by the U.S. Department of Education completed in 1999 documented this and highlighted some of the major obstacles at the beginning stages of development. The study identified financial difficulties as being among the largest problems, although there has been a marked decline over time in the percentage of schools facing problems with start-up funding.

In addition to financial issues, newly created schools were likely to face difficulties with lack of start-up planning time, inadequate facilities, internal conflicts, school administration and management, teacher turnover, community opposition, and communication with parents. Let's look at some of these challenges a bit closer.

In the chartering process itself, the applicants may meet resistance from the community, the local school district, the unions or bargaining units operating in the area schools, and the state department of education. All of these forms of resistance have become less difficult to address as the charter school movement itself has built up a successful record. Much has been written about local school board opposition to charter schools. In my observations, however, school boards tend to go along with the state governing authority once a state legislature decides to allow charter schools. Although most local school boards feel threatened by these schools coming into their districts, they generally back off with a sort of benign neglect toward charter schools. Once a charter school opens, whatever opposition exists manifests itself in a lack of help or services to the school.

In the early days of set-up and operations, the founders are likely to disagree with one another. Frustrations and tensions are normal as individuals work to meet deadlines, to bring the school into existence, and to establish a smoothly functioning organization. These are struggles common to all start-up processes, not just charter schools. Most organizations continue to encounter them from time to time, even after they are well established.

Without a doubt, one of the most complicated issues every charter school must face involves locating and maintaining suitable physical facilities. Once a group is granted the charter, it

Start-Up Problems Encountered by Charter Schools

Problem/Difficulty	Percentage Reporting the Problem
Lack of start-up funds	53.7%
Inadequate operating funds	40.4%
Lack of planning time	37.4%
Inadequate facilities	35.4%
State or local board opposition	20.4%
District resistance or regulations	19.0%
State Department of Education resistance	11.3%
Internal processes or conflicts	13.1%
School administration and management	12.4%
Health and safety regulations	11.9%
Hiring staff	10.6%
Teacher burnout	10.6%
Accountability requirements	8.2%
Lack of parental support	8.4%
Union or bargaining unit opposition	7.5%
Teacher certification requirements	6.0%
Teacher turnover	6.6%
Collective bargaining agreements	4.2%
Community opposition	5.9%
Communication with parents	5.3%
Federal regulations	4.5%

U.S. Department of Education Study, 1999

often runs into major difficulties finding an adequate facility. Whether the founding group leases, buys, or builds a building, a school needs a place to call home. Some charter schools have developed highly creative solutions to the problem of facilities, converting storefronts or sharing space with other organizations.

After the school's initial facilities problem is solved, many face a new problem a few years later. Since most charter schools start small and grow a grade or two per year, they don't need more space until three to four years down the road. Then, when the school has become a success in the eyes of the public, more and more parents want to enroll their children. The charter school then has a waiting list of students that it can't possibly admit due to the facilities limitations. I know of several charter schools that are only able to admit sixteen to twenty-four new students a year due to lack of space. In time, the problem of space limitations begins to defeat the very purpose of the charter school, which is to help families in the local community gain access to a better education for their children.

But of all the struggles and obstacles start-up charter schools face, funding is the most common and often the most challenging. Many charter schools start up and operate on shoestring budgets. And many do so with far greater success than do neighboring public schools with more generous funding. Nevertheless, all schools need money, and charter schools are no exception. Schools need money to do the simplest things—to lease or purchase a building; to equip the building with lights, chalkboards, and desks; to obtain books and supplies for teachers and students; and to pay teachers and administrators, to list just a few of the more obvious expenses. Lack of money, and specifically lack of start-up funds, is the key reason some charter schools fail and many others never get off the ground in the first place.

In his book, *Charter Schools, Another Flawed Educational Reform* (Teachers College Press, 1998), Seymour B. Sarason states, "Several of the school leaders and founders complained that inadequate start-up funding was a difficulty in the early stages of the school development. At most schools, staff could not be hired until shortly before the school opened, as there were not enough funds to pay salaries over the summer."

I am certain that lack of funding affects the ability of some charter schools to get things off the ground the first year, but many schools have found ingenious ways to get around these issues. Because charter schools are innovative, many are able to encourage teachers and other staff members to defer parts of their salaries in the beginning. Some administrators and staff members contribute some of their time and effort freely during start-up. In addition, many charter schools receive lots of practical support from the community, as parents and other volunteers provide free labor in helping to build parts of the structure of the building where the school is located.

Some charter schools contract out the work that only a skilled laborer can do but ask parents, staff, students, and community members to come in to paint and do nonskilled work for free. Many are more than willing to do this as a way to show support for the school. Ultimately, this kind of support creates a sense of camaraderie in the school and the school's community, which translates into an atmosphere of warmth and cooperation inside the school building. The charter schools that manage to engage people in such ways get much more support from the community in other ways as the school endures.

One promising development in the financial area involves continuing interest and support of the federal government. In his Call to Action for American Education in the Twenty-First Century, President Clinton made charter schools and the funding to support them a key feature of his education plan. For fiscal year 1999 alone, Congress appropriated $100 million for start-up grants to charter schools.

Thus we see that, for each and every obstacle charter schools face, people find solutions and move forward. The entire choice movement and charter school movement rest on just that "can do" spirit.

Appendix I

SOME BASIC FACTS AND FIGURES

I N LESS THAN a decade, charter schools have gone from nonexistent to widespread. In 1991, Minnesota became the first state to enact charter school legislation. By July 1996, twenty-five states had enacted varying forms of charter school laws. And by the end of 1999, almost three-quarters of the states had charter school enabling laws on their books. Specifically, today, thirty-six states, the District of Columbia, and Puerto Rico have all passed charter school laws. The thirty-six states are Alaska, Arkansas, Arizona, California, Colorado, Connecticut, Delaware, Florida, Georgia, Hawaii, Idaho, Illinois, Kansas, Louisiana, Massachusetts, Michigan, Minnesota, Missouri, Mississippi, North Carolina, New Hampshire, New Jersey, New Mexico, Nevada, New York, Ohio, Oklahoma, Oregon, Pennsylvania, Rhode Island, South Carolina, Texas, Utah, Virginia, Wisconsin, and Wyoming.

As the enabling laws have been passed, charter schools have been founded apace. At the beginning of 1996, 252 charter schools were operating in 10 states. In that year alone, almost

Table A1.1   Growth of Charter Schools in the U.S., 1992–2000

State	92–93	93–94	94–95	95–96	96–97	97–98	98–99	99–2000	Total
Minnesota	2	5	7	3	3	8	12	17	**54**
California		28	36	30	21	19	29	9	**210**
Colorado		1	13	10	8	19	10	1	**68**
Michigan			2	41	33	36	24	5	**146**
New Mexico			4	0	1	0	0	3	**3**
Wisconsin			2	3	6	7	12	11	**40**
Arizona				47	58	45	44	44	**222**
Georgia				3	9	9	7	4	**31**
Hawaii				2	0	0	0	0	**2**
Massachusetts				15	7	3	10	5	**39**
Alaska					2	13	2	1	**18**
Delaware					2	1	1	1	**5**
Washington, D.C.					2	1	17	10	**28**
Florida					5	28	42	4	**109**
Illinois					1	7	6	7	**20**
Louisiana					3	3	5	7	**18**
Texas					17	21	71	64	**168**

Connecticut	12	4	2	17
Kansas	1	14	0	15
New Jersey	13	17	0	49
North Carolina	34	26	23	78
Pennsylvania	6	25	17	48
Rhode Island	1	1	0	2
South Carolina	2	3	5	10
Idaho		2	6	8
Mississippi		1	0	1
Nevada		1	0	1
Ohio		15	31	46
New York			5	5
Missouri			15	15
Utah			6	6
Oklahoma			2	2

U.S. Department of Education's National Study of Charter Schools, 2000

140 additional schools opened. In 1999, 421 new charter schools opened, bringing the 1999–2000 total to 1,484 charter schools. And the pace shows no signs of slowing.

Table A1.1 illustrates the growth of the charter school movement from 1992 forward.

Number of Charter Schools Allowed to Open per State

THE NUMBER OF charter schools allowed to open varies from state to state. Many states have no limitations at all, while others have limitations based on state caps or local school district caps. Thirteen of the thirty-seven chartering jurisdictions (thirty-six states plus the District of Columbia) place no limit on the number of charter schools allowed to open. The state of Virginia allows only 2 charter schools per school district, and the state of New Jersey allows 135 charter schools overall. The remaining twenty-two jurisdictions either limit the total number of charter schools allowed by district or the number of new schools allowed to open per year. While states initially put caps on the number of charter schools allowed to open, as the charter school momentum picks up across the United States, more and more states are lifting these initial caps.

Arizona leads the nation in number of charter schools, with nearly 350 schools in operation, followed by California (234), Michigan (over 175), Texas (over 150), and Florida (112).

Table A1.2 provides a rundown on the current limitations, state by state.

Estimated Charter School Enrollment

ALTHOUGH SOME STATES have placed caps on the number of charter schools that can open, they have not limited the

Table A1.2 Number of Charter Schools Allowed by State

State	Number of Schools Allowed to Open
Alaska	30
Arizona	No limit
Arkansas	No limit
California	100 annually
Colorado	No limit
Connecticut	24
Delaware	No limit
Florida	Special limitations
Georgia	No limit
Hawaii	25
Idaho	60
Illinois	45
Kansas	15
Louisiana	42
Massachusetts	50
Michigan	No limit
Minnesota	No limit
Mississippi	6
Missouri	Special limitations
Nevada	Special limitations
New Hampshire	10 annually
New Jersey	135
New Mexico	20 annually
New York	100 new, unlimited public conversion
North Carolina	100
Ohio	No limit
Oklahoma	Special limitations
Oregon	Special limitations
Pennsylvania	No limit
Rhode Island	20
South Carolina	No limit
Texas	No limit
Utah	8
Virginia	2 per district
Washington, D.C.	20 annually
Wisconsin	No limit
Wyoming	No limit

U.S. Department of Education, Charter Schools Third-Year Report, 1999.

number of students who can enroll in each school. Student enrollment has been brisk, with the majority of charter schools running a waiting list of students who wish to enroll.

The number of students in charter schools increased in the 1998–1999 school year by nearly 90,000, bringing the total to more than 250,000 students. This total represents 0.8 percent of all public school students in states with open charter schools as of the 1998–1999 school year. With 73,905 students in charter schools, California had the largest number of charter school students of any state. Three states together—Arizona, California, and Michigan—account for more than half of all charter school student enrollments (52 percent).

The Center for Education Reform estimated that, by the fall of 1999, 350,000 students either were attending or had previously attended charter schools in the United States.

Table A1.3 shows the estimated student enrollment, state by state, for the 1998–1999 school year.

Size of Average Charter School

MOST CHARTER SCHOOLS are small schools with a median enrollment of approximately 137 students. Nearly half have a grade configuration that deviates from the traditional public elementary, middle, and high school configuration. In 1998–1999, one-quarter of the charter schools spanned K–8 or K–12.

Student-to-Teacher Ratio

THE MEDIAN STUDENT-to-teacher ratio for charter schools is sixteen students per teacher, which is slightly lower than the ratio for all public schools of seventeen students per teacher.

Ethnic/Racial Composition

JUST AS CHARTER school enrollment varies according to school, the ethnic composition of schools varies as well.

Table A1.3   Estimated Number of Students Enrolled in Charter Schools by State, 1998–1999

State	Charter School Enrollment
Alaska	2,047
Arizona	32,209
California	73,905
Colorado	13,911
Connecticut	1,613
Delaware	988
Florida	10,561
Georgia	18,611
Hawaii	790
Idaho	57
Illinois	3,333
Kansas	1,545
Louisiana	1,589
Massachusetts	9,673
Michigan	25,294
Minnesota	4,670
Mississippi	340
New Jersey	4,001
New Mexico	4,601
North Carolina	9,513
Ohio	2,509
Pennsylvania	5,474
Rhode Island	397
South Carolina	364
Texas	18,590
Washington, D.C.	3,364
Wisconsin	2,060
Total	**252,009**

U.S. Department of Education, Charter Schools Third-Year Report, 1999.

According to the U.S. Department of Education National Study of Charter Schools, overall, charter schools currently enroll a larger percentage of students of color than all public schools in the states with charter schools in operation. On average, charter schools enrolled a lower percentage of white students (50 percent versus 63 percent) and a larger percentage of black students (27 percent versus 17 percent) than all public schools in the charter states. The percentage of white students in charter schools declined from 52 percent in the 1996–1997 school year to about 48 percent in the 1998–1999 school year.

Charter schools in several states—Connecticut, Illinois, Louisiana, Massachusetts, Michigan, Minnesota, New Jersey, North Carolina, and Texas—enroll a much larger percentage of students of color than all public schools in those states. Charter schools in Alaska, California, and Georgia serve a higher proportion of white students than do all public schools in those states.

For more information on the racial makeup of charter schools, state by state, see table A1.4.

Accountability of Charter Schools

ALTHOUGH CHARTER SCHOOLS have considerable autonomy, they are held accountable to provide financial and student achievement reports to different constituencies. The majority of charter schools control most areas critical to school operations, including purchasing, hiring, scheduling, and curriculum.

More than nine of ten charter schools were monitored for accountability in terms of school finances; nearly nine of ten for student achievement and for compliance with regulations; more than eight of ten for student attendance; and more than six of ten for instructional practices.

Table A1.4 Racial Makeup of Charter Schools, by State

State	Number of Schools	% White	% Black	% Hispanic	% Asian
Alaska	13	70.7	2.6	2.6	1.0
Arizona	155	46.9	2.5	1.7	2.7
California	143	54.5	10.8	26.6	4.4
Colorado	57	76.6	6.0	14.0	2.0
Connecticut	16	32.5	45.0	21.0	1.0
Delaware	4	56.3	39.0	2.6	2.2
Florida	60	48.8	40.3	9.6	0.5
Georgia	25	69.6	23.4	3.4	2.1
Illinois	11	8.6	67.0	23.2	1.0
Kansas	14	90.2	1.2	6.4	0.5
Louisiana	10	25.0	72.4	0.4	0.7
Massachusetts	32	58.0	20.1	13.8	2.0
Michigan	121	50.0	41.4	4.6	0.8
Minnesota	37	51.9	26.7	3.4	10.3
New Jersey	21	20.6	62.1	13.5	3.3
New Mexico	5	35.3	2.1	56.8	1.3
North Carolina	51	48.4	47.3	1.6	0.6
Ohio	7	44.1	49.8	1.0	0.0
Pennsylvania	22	25.1	59.1	13.8	1.8
South Carolina	4	23.1	72.3	0.0	0.0
Texas	72	23.1	33.9	39.5	2.5
Washington, D.C.	14	1.0	74.3	19.9	3.6
Wisconsin	26	72.6	16.0	2.7	2.8

U.S. Department of Education, National Center for
Education Statistics, Common Core of Data Survey, 1997–98.

The charter school states differ greatly in how they approach accountability, with some following a centralized state agency approach, others a market-driven approach, and still others a district-based approach that relies on local accountability within a framework of state testing.

Accountability for Students' Progress

More than nine of ten charter schools used student achievement tests, augmented by other measures of student performance and school success, to report to their chartering agency, the school's governing board, and/or parents. More than one-third of charter schools used at least seven measures of school performance, including standardized tests and other measures of student achievement, parent and student surveys, and behavioral indicators.

Family Interest and Satisfaction

PARENTS REPORT THAT their main reasons for choosing charter schools are small size, better quality education, and more desirable educational philosophies. Students mention good teachers and good teaching as primary advantages in their charter schools, while weak programming in sports and other extracurricular activities bring some criticism from the youngsters in charter schools.

For more information on reasons for choosing charter schools and on satisfaction, see table A1.5 and table A1.6.

Table A1.5   Reasons Parents Chose Charter Schools

Reason	Percentage
Small size of charter school	53.0
Higher standards at charter school	45.9
Program closer to my educational philosophy	44.0
Greater opportunity for parent involvement	43.0
Better teachers at charter school	41.9
Unhappy with curriculum/teachers at former charter school	34.5
My child wanted to come here	30.3
Location of charter school more convenient	29.5
Charter school offers a before/after school	24.3
People told me this is a better school	21.8
Previous school was unsafe	20.1
My child's special needs not met at last school	19.9
Prefer private school but could not afford	18.7
My child was doing badly in regular school	16.9

Finn, Manno, Bierlein, and Vanourek, 1997

Table A1.6   Students' Charter School Likes and Dislikes

Likes	Percentage	Dislikes	Percentage
Good teachers	58.6	Poor sports program	29.4
Teach it until I learn it	51.3	Not enough other activities	29.4
Don't let me fall behind	38.5	Food	28.6
Computer & technology	35.7	Too much homework	28.5
Nice people running the school	34.9	Boring	23.4
Teacher's attention	33.9	Not enough computers	21.8
Curriculum	33.3	Too strict	19.7
Safety	27.5	Difficult commute	14.5
School size	25.4	Poor facilities	12.1
A lot is expected of me	19.7	Bad teachers	9.1
Parents get to participate	15.9	Not enough homework	6.9
Sports programs	15.8	Classes too big/small	6.7
Food	12.0	Too tough academically	6.7
		Not safe enough	6.3
		Not strict enough	6.0

Finn, Manno, Bierlein, and Vanourek, 1997

Appendix II

FOR MORE INFORMATION

State Charter Granting Agencies, Web Sites, and Publications

THIS APPENDIX LISTS additional resources and information sources for a parent interested in learning more about charter schools, in finding one in a particular area or investigating a particular charter school, or, finally, in founding a new charter school. First, you'll find a complete list of the state agencies in charge of granting charters and overseeing the schools. If your state has enacted charter school legislation, the agency can answer your questions and tell you about schools in your area and the process for chartering a school in your state.

Following the agency listing, you will find a selected listing of Web sites with information and discussion of charter schools and the charter school movement. For each of the site listings, I have provided some information about the site itself or the organization owning the site.

Finally, this appendix concludes with a list of print references. More than a hundred articles and multiple books have

175

been written about charter schools. As a parent who's interested in sending your child to a charter school, you should become as knowledgeable as possible. To help you build your knowledge, I have selected thirty-seven books, monographs, articles, and other publications that I believe might be interesting and useful to you.

State Charter-Granting Agencies

Alaska
Charter School Liaison
Alaska Department of Education
801 West 10th Street
Juneau, AK 99801-1894
(907) 465-8720

Arizona
Charter School Board Director
Arizona Department of Education
1535 West Jefferson Street
Phoenix, AZ 85007
(602) 542-3411

Arkansas
Director of Charter Schools
State of Arkansas, Department of Education
#4 State Capitol Mall
Little Rock, AR 72201
(501) 682-4251

California
Charter Schools Office
Department of Education
721 Capitol Mall
Sacramento, CA 95814
(916) 327-5929

Colorado
Charter School Priority Project Team
Colorado Department of Education
201 East Colfax
Denver, CO 80203-1799
(303) 866-6631

Connecticut
Charter Schools Program Manager
Connecticut Department of Education
165 Capitol Avenue
State Office Building
Hartford, CT 06106-1630
(860) 566-1233

Delaware
Charter School Administrator
Delaware Department of Public Information
P.O. Box 1402
Dover, DE 19903
(302) 739-4885

Florida
Florida Department of Education
PL-08, The Capitol
Tallahassee, FL 32399
(904) 413-9707

Georgia
Georgia Department of Education
1866 Twin Towers East
Atlanta, GA 30334
(404) 656-0630

Hawaii

Charter School Administrator
Hawaii Department of Education
1270 Queen Emma Street #409
Honolulu, HI 96813
(808) 586-3124

Illinois

Illinois State Department of Education
100 North First Street
Springfield, IL 62777
(217) 782-5270

Kansas

Charter School Administrator
Kansas State Department of Education
120 East 10th Street
Topeka, KS 66612
(913) 296-3204

Louisiana

Charter School Administrator
Louisiana State Department of Education
P.O. Box 94064
626 North Fourth Street, 12th Floor
Baton Rouge, LA 70804-9064
(504) 324-3603

Massachusetts

Associate Commissioner for Charter Schools
Massachusetts Department of Education
1 Ashburton Place, Room 1401
Boston, MA 02108
(617) 727-0075

Michigan
Charter School Administrator
Michigan State Department of Education
P.O. Box 30008
608 Allegan Street
Lansing, MI 48909
(517) 373-4631

Minnesota
Charter Schools Administrator
Minnesota State Department of Education
712 Capitol Square Building
550 Cedar Street
St. Paul, MN 55101
(612) 296-4213

Mississippi
Charter School Consultant
P.O. Box 771
Jackson, MS 39055
(601) 359-3501

Missouri
Department of Elementary Education
P.O. Box 480
Jefferson, MO 65102
(314) 751-3175

Nevada
Nevada Department of Education
700 East Fifth Street
Carson City, NV 89701-5906
(702) 687-9158

New Hampshire
Administrator for Legislative Affairs
New Hampshire Department of Education
State Office Park South
101 Pleasant Street
Concord, NH 03301
(603) 271-3879

New Jersey
Director of Innovative Programs
New Jersey State Department of Education
225 West State Street, CN 500
Trenton, NJ 08625-0500
(609) 292-5850

New Mexico
Charter School Administrator
New Mexico State Department of Education
300 Don Gaspar Drive
Santa Fe, NM 87501-2786
(505) 827-6576

North Carolina
Charter School Office
North Carolina Department of Public Instruction
Education Building
301 North Wilmington Street
Raleigh, NC 27601-2825
(919) 715-1730

Ohio
Ohio Department of Education
65 South Front Street, Room 408
Columbus, OH 43215
(614) 466-2937

Pennsylvania
Policy Specialist
Pennsylvania Department of Education
Policy Office
333 Market Street, 10th Floor
Harrisburg, PA 17126-0333
(717) 783-9781

Rhode Island
Charter School Administrator
Rhode Island Department of Education
Sheperd Building
255 Westminster Street
Providence, RI 02903-3400
(401) 277-4600, ext. 2209

South Carolina
Special Assistant-Policy
Department of Education
1429 Senate Street, Room 1005
Columbia, SC 29201
(803) 734-8500

Texas
Charter School Administrator
Texas Education Agency
William B. Travis Building
1701 North Travis Building
Austin, TX 78701-1494
(512) 463-9575

Washington, D.C.
Charter Schools Administrator
DC Public Schools
405 12th Street NW
Washington, DC 20004
(202) 724-2406

Wisconsin
Wisconsin Department of Education
P.O. Box 7841
Madison, WI 53707
(608) 266-5728

Wyoming
Charter School Administrator
Wyoming State Department of Education
2300 Capitol Avenue
2nd Floor, Hathaway Building
Cheyenne, WY 82002
(307) 777-6268

Web Sites for Additional Charter School Information

Center for Education Reform   www.edreform.com
The Center for Educational Reform provides information on the charter school movement. It also maintains a national charter school directory and national summary and charter school statistics.

Center for School Change
www.hhh.umn.edu/centers/school-change/
The Center for School Change offers on-line research and helpful information on charter schools and related topics.

Educational Excellence Network   www.edexcellence.net
The Educational Excellence Network offers on-line some of the most recent and significant research performed on charter school–related issues.

Education Week on the Web
www.edweek.org/context/topics/issues.cfm

Web site of an independent weekly newspaper that covers elementary and secondary education.

Institute for Education Reform's Charter School's Development Center
www.csus.edu/ier/charter/charter.html

The Institute for Education Reform's Charter School's Development Center provides a substantial amount of information and guidance on setting up and running a charter school. While some of the material is California-specific, much can be adapted to charter school operators in any other state.

Manhattan Institute's Center for Charter Schools
www.manhattaninstitute.org

The Manhattan Institute's Center for Charter Schools provides information about charter schools.

Michigan Resource Center for Charter Schools
www.charter.ehhs.cmich.edu

The Michigan Resource Center for Charter Schools provides information about charter schools in the state of Michigan.

Pioneer Institute's Charter School Resource Center
www.pioneerinstitute.org/csrc

The Pioneer Institute Charter School Resource Center provides up-to-date information on the development and support of charter schools in and outside of the state of Massachusetts. The center has an online Massachusetts Charter School Handbook, which offers comprehensive technical assistance for starting a charter school in or outside of the state of Massachusetts.

U.S. Charter Schools Web Site   www.uscharterschools.org
Sponsored by the U.S. Department of Education, WestEd, and the Institute for Educational Reform at California State University, this site features far-reaching information on charter schools in the United States. It offers guidelines for establishing a charter school, research references on charter schools, and a contact list of existing charter schools. It also provides an opportunity to join discussion groups with others interested in the charter school movement.

Published Reference Material

The Third-Year Report of the National Study of Charter Schools, **May 1999, U.S. Department of Education**
Examines trends among charter schools in operation during the 1997–1998 school year.

Steps to Starting a Charter School, **March 1999**
An overview of the process of founding a charter school, from U.S. Charter Schools. This includes URLs for reports and research on charter schools.

Grants to States for Charter Schools
Basic facts about funds available to states from the U.S. Department of Education to establish charter schools.

Charter School Research
A public space dedicated to charter schools. It provides a catalog of charter school–related materials and enables "inquiry, communication, critique, and justifiable experimentation."

The Massachusetts Charter School Initiative 1997–98 Report
A summary of annual reports, supplemented with information from reports required of all public schools, including charter schools, from the Massachusetts Department of Education.

Paying for the Charter Schoolhouse: A Policy Agenda for Charter School Facilities Financing, January 1999

Charter School Finance: Policies, Activities and Challenges in Four States, November 1997
A policy brief from the Education Commission of the States looks at financial issues for charter schools in Arizona, California, Massachusetts, and Michigan and selected schools within those states. See also ECS's issue brief on charter schools in general.

Charters in Our Midst: The Impact of Charter Schools on School Districts, A Roadmap to What Lies Ahead, 1997
The North Central Regional Educational Laboratory Policy Publications.

The U.S. Department of Education's Charter Schools Demonstration Program, March 17, 1995

Minnesota Charter Schools Evaluation: Interim Report, December 1996
A study of Minnesota charter schools from the University of Minnesota.

The Charter Movement: Education Reform School by School, 1996
A report on charter schools from California's Little Hoover Commission.

Charter Schools in Action: What Have We Learned? 1996
A report from the Hudson Institute that describes a survey of thirty-five schools and site visits to forty-three schools in seven states.

Charter Schools: New Model for Public Schools Provides Opportunities and Challenges
A report from the U.S. General Accounting Office.

Charter School Laws: Do They Measure Up? 1996
A report from the American Federation of Teachers that endorses charter schools as useful vehicles for school reform, if they can demonstrate improved student achievement.

Additional Published Material

Allen, J. (1995) *Nine Lies About School Choice, Answering the Critics.* Washington, D.C.: Center for Education Reform.

Amsler, M., & L. Mulholland. (1992). *Charter Schools.* San Francisco: Far West Laboratory for Educational Research and Development.

Bierlein, L. A., & M. Bateman. (1998). Opposition forces and education reform: Will charter schools succeed? *Network News & Views* 14(11): 682–688.

Bierlein, L. A., & L. Mulholland. (1993). *Charter School Update: Expansion of a Viable Reform Initiative.* Tempe: School of Public Affairs, Arizona State University.

Bomotti, Sally. (1996, October). Why do parents choose alternative schools? *Educational Leadership,* 54(2).

Broderick, C. (1995). Rocky Mountain rift: In the Mile-High City of Denver, a maverick school board challenges the state's charter school law. *American School Board Journal* 182(10): 32–34.

Budde, Ray. (1996, September). The evolution of the charter concept. *Phi Delta Kappan* 78(1).

Corwin, R. G., & J. F. Flaherty. (eds.). (1995). *Freedom and Innovation in California's Charter Schools.* Los Alamitos, CA: Southwest Regional Educational Laboratory.

Cutter, Milo. (1996, September). City Academy. *Phi Delta Kappan* 78(1).

Dale, A. H. (ed.). (1996). *National Charter School Directory,* 3rd ed. Washington, D.C.: Center for Education Reform.

Dianda, M., & R. Corwin. (1994). *Vision and Reality: A First-Year Look at California's Charter Schools*. Los Alamitos, CA: Southwest Regional Educational Laboratory.

Education Commission of the States. (1995). *Charter Schools: What Are They Up To? A 1995 Survey.* Denver, CO: Author.

Education Industry Report. (1996). *Charter Laws: What They Mean for the Industry.* St. Cloud, MN: Author.

Fine, M. (1993). *Democratizing choice: Reinventing Public Education.* New York: CUNY Graduate Center.

Finn, C. E., Jr., B. V. Manno, L. A. Bierlein, and G. Vanourek. (1996). *Charter Schools in Action: What Have We Learned?* Indianapolis: The Hudson Institute.

Goenner, James. (1996, September). Charter schools: The revitalization of public education. *Phi Delta Kappan* 78(1).

Little Hoover Commission. (1996). *The Charter Movement: Education Reform School by School.* Sacramento, CA: Author.

McKinney, Joseph R. (1996, October). Charter schools: A new barrier for children with disabilities. *Educational Leadership,* 54(2).

Molnar, Alex. (1996, October). Charter schools: The smiling face of disinvestment. *Educational Leadership,* 54(2).

Myatt, Larry, & Nathan, Linda. (1996, September). One school's journey in the Age of Reform. *Phi Delta Kappan* 78(1).

Nathan, J., & J. Ysseldyke. (1994). What Minnesota has learned about school choice. *Phi Delta Kappan* 75(9), 682–688.

Nathan, Joe. (1996, September). Possibilities, problems, and progress: Early lessons for the charter movement. *Phi Delta Kappan* 78(1).

O'Neil, John. (1996, October). New options, old concerns. *Educational Leadership,* 54(2).

Page, Linda, with Mark Levine. (1996, October). The pitfalls and triumphs of launching a charter school. *Educational Leadership,* 54(2).

Premack, E. (1996, September). The story of California's education reform: Power tool. *Phi Delta Kappan* 78(1).

Randall, W. T. (1996). *Charter Schools: What Colorado Has Learned Over the Past Two Years*. Alexandria, VA: National School Boards Association.

Thomas, Doug, & Kim Borwege. (1996, September). A choice to charter. *Phi Delta Kappan* 78(1).

U.S. General Accounting Office (1995, January). *Charter Schools: A Growing and Diverse National Reform Movement* (Report No. GAO/T-HEHS-95-52). Washington, D.C.: Author.

Wagner, Tony. (1996, September). School choice: To what end? *Phi Delta Kappan* 78(1).

Young, T. W., & D. Mah. (1994, Fall). Bowling Green elementary charter school. *New Schools, New Communities* 11(1): 21–25.

Appendix III

COMPLETE LIST OF EXISTING
AND NEWLY APPROVED
CHARTER SCHOOLS

THE FOLLOWING LIST includes charter schools in the United States, organized alphabetically by state.

A list of schools approved but not open as of the fall of 2000 begins on page 222.

Alaska

Academy Charter School
641 Cope Industrial Way
Palmer, AK 99645

Aurora Borealis Charter School
34640 Kalifornsky Beach Road
Soldotna, AK 99669

Bay View Charter School
Box 3313
Seward, AK 99664

Family Partnership Charter School
3339 Fairbanks Street
Anchorage, AK 99503

Juneau Community Charter School
430 Fourth Street
Juneau, AK 99801

Ketchikan Charter School
630 North Point Higgens Road
Ketchikan, AK 99901

Midnight Sun Family Learning Center
PO Box 878629
Wasilla, AK 99687-8629

New Beginnings Charter School
P.O. Box 70219
Fairbanks, AK 99707

Project Education Charter School
Galena High School
P.O. Box 359
Galena, AK 99741

**Takotna Training Center—
Charter School**
General Delivery, Mile 412,
Iditarod Trail
Takotna, AK 99675

Village Charter School
P.O. Box 190051
Anchorage, AK 99519

Walden Pond Charter School
800 E. Dimond Blvd., #3-209
Anchorage, AK 99519

Arizona

ACCLAIM Charter School
5350 West Indian School Road
Phoenix, AZ 85031

**Alternative Learning Charter
School Benson**
248 Fourth Street
Benzon, AZ 85602

**Arizona Agribusiness
and Equine Center**
Phoenix, AZ

**Arizona Montessori Charter
School**
7555 Long Look Drive
Prescott Valley, AZ 85015

**Benjamin Fanklin Charter
School—Gilbert Campus**
13732 East Warner Road
Gilbert, AZ 85296

Bryan Charter Schools
Prescott Valley
Peoria, AZ 82070

Calli Ollin Academy
1525 N. Orcle Road, Suite 107
Tucson, AZ 85705

**Carmel Community Arts and
Technology**
97 West Oakland Street
Chandler, AZ 85224

**Carmel Community
Integrated Arts**
325 Arizona Street
Bisbee, AZ 85603

Central City Academy
4530 North Central Avenue
Phoenix, AZ 85012

Challenge Charter School
16635 North 51st Avenue
Glendale, AZ 85306

Classical Kids' Academy
6437 West Chandler Boulevard
Chandler, AZ 85226

Desert Eagle Secondary School
3191 North Longmore
Scottsdale, AZ 85256

Desert Springs Scholastic Institute
745 North Gilbert Road
Suite 124-314
Gilbert, AZ 85234

Dobson Academy
2207 North Dobson Road
Chandler, AZ 85224

**Downtown Community
Charter School**
110 South Church Avenue #1160
Tucson, AZ 85701

**EcoTech Agricultural Charter
School**
12221 East Pecos Road
Chandler, AZ 85225

EduPreneurship Student Center
1201 North 85th Place
Scottsdale, AZ 85257

Excalibur Charter School
8320 East Baseline Avenue
Mesa, AZ 85208

EXCEL High School
1987 McCulloch Boulevard,
Suite 203
Lake Havasu, AZ 86403

**Flagstaff Arts & Leadership
Academy**
3100 North Fort Valley Road, #41
Flagstaff, AZ 86001

Foothills Academy
6424 East Cave Creek Road
Cave Creek, AZ 85331

Fountain Hills Charter School
15055 North Fountain Hills
Boulevard
Fountain Hills, AZ 85268

**GateWay Community High
School**
108 North 40th Street
Phoenix, AZ 85034-1795

GEM Charter School
1704 North Center Street
Mesa, AZ 85201

Genesis Academy
640 North 1st Avenue
Phoenix, AZ 85003

Greyhills Academy High School
P.O. Box 160
Warrior Drive
Tuba City, AZ 86045

**Ha:san Preparatory
and Leadership School**
1333 East 10th Street
Tucson, AZ 85719

Hearn Academy
1055 East Hearn Road
Phoenix, AZ 85022

**Hermosa Montessori
Charter School**
12051 East Fort Lowell
Tucson, AZ 85749

Horizon Charter School—Phoenix
2420 East Liberty Lane
Phoenix, AZ 85048

Humanities and Sciences Institute
5201 North 7th Street
Phoenix, AZ 85014

Intelli-School Charter High School
3101 West Peoria Avenue,
Suite B310
Phoenix, AZ 85029

International Studies Academy
4744 West Grovers
Glendale, AZ 85308

**Jurisprudence Charter
School, The**
927 West Javalina Street
Mesa, AZ 85210

Kingman Academy of Learning
1910 East Andy Devine Avenue
Kingman, AZ 86401

Lake Havasu Charter School
1055 Empire Drive
Lake Havasu City, AZ 86404

Liberty High School
482 Hagen Road
Globe, AZ 85501

Life School College Preparatory
2830 Brown Road, #A
Mesa, AZ 85213

Looking Glass School, The
15030 North 64th Street
Scottsdale, AZ 85254

Mexicaytl Charter School
590 North Morley Avenue
Nogales, AZ 85821

New School for the Arts
7475 East McDowell Road
Scottsdale, AZ 85257

PACE Preparatory Academy
460 South Main Street
Camp Verde, AZ 86322

Paradise Education Center
155533 West Paradise Lane
Surprise, AZ 85374

Park View Middle School
8300 East Dana Drive
Prescott Valley, AZ 86303

Pine Forest Charter School
1120 West Kaibab Lane
Flagstaff, AZ 86001

PPEP TEC Charter High Schools
(System-12 sites)
Tucson, AZ 85713

Presidio School
4601 East First Street
Tucson, AZ 85711

Primeria Alta High School
310 North Grand Court Plaza Drive
Nogales, AZ 85621

Scottsdale Institute for the Arts
5025 North Central Avenue, #426
Phoenix, AZ 85012

Sedona Charter School
3270 White Bear Road
Sedona, AZ 86336

Sequoia Schools
1460 South Home
Mesa, AZ 85204

Skyview School
Rush Street
Prescott, AZ 86301

Sonoran Desert School
4448 East Main Street, Suite 7
Mesa, AZ 85207

Telesis Learning Center
2598 Starlite Lane
Lake Havasu City, AZ 86403

California

Academy for Academic Excellence
20720 Thunderbird Road
Apple Valley, CA 92307

Academy for Career Education
715 13th Street
Modesto, CA 95354

Academy for Career Education
801 Olive Street
Wheatland, CA 95692

Accelerated Charter School
116 E. Martin Luther King
Boulevard
Los Angeles, CA 90011

Advanced Instructional
Model Charter School
9055 Locust Street
Elk Grove, CA 95624

Alianza School
440 Arthur Road
Watsonville, CA 95076

Art's Charter School
2350 Beverly Drive
Redding, CA 96002

Aurora High School (a Bay
Area Charter High School)
P.O. Box 822
San Carlos, CA 94070

Baldwin Hills Charter/LEARN
Elementary & Magnet
5421 Rodeo Road
Los Angeles, CA 90016

Bellevue—
Santa Fe Charter School
1401 San Luis Bay Drive
San Luis Obispo, CA 93405

Bitney Springs
Charter High School
P.O. Box 255
Grass Valley, CA 95949

Black Oak Charter School
P.O. Box 339
c/o Guidiville Indian Rancheria
Talmange, CA 95481

Bowling Green Charter
4211 Turnbridge Drive
Sacramento, CA 95823

Cali Calmecac Charter School
9291 Old Redwood Highway, 300c
Windsor, CA 95492

California Charter Academy
12530 Hesperia Road, Suite 209
Victorville, CA 92392

Camptonville Academy, The
P.O. Box 218
15464 Cleveland Avenue
Camptonville, CA 95922

Canyon Charter School
421 Entrada Drive
Santa Monica, CA 90402

Challenge Charter High School
2425 Myers Street
Oroville, CA 95966

Challenge Youth
Program Charter School
P.O. Box 8105
San Luis Obispo, CA 93403

Charter 101
12408 Hesperia Road, Suite 9 & 10
Victorville, CA 92392

Charter Alternatives Academy
6832 Avenue 280
Visalia, CA 93277

Charter Community School
and Extended Day Program
6767 Green Valley Road
Placerville, CA 95667

Charter Early Kindergarten
505 Main Street
Nevada City, CA 95959

Charter Home School Academy
6600 West Hurley
Visalia, CA 93291

Charter Oak School
211 West Tulare Avenue
Visalia, CA 93277

Charter School of San Diego, The
2245 San Diego Avenue, Suite 127
San Diego, CA 92110

Children's Community Charter
School
5665 Recreation Drive
Paradise, CA 95969

Choice 2000 Online Charter
School
146 East 4th Street
Perris, CA 92570

Chrysalis Charter School
1155 Mistletoe Lane
Redding CA 96002

Chula Vista Learning
Community Charter School
939 4th Avenue
Chula Vista, CA 91911

Citrus Heights Charter School
P.O. Box 4557
Citrus Heights, CA 95611

Clear View Charter Elementary
455 Windrose Way
Chula Vista, CA 91910

Community Charter Middle
School
San Fernando, CA 91340

Country Charter School
P.O. Box 918
Occidental, CA 95645

Creative Arts Charter School
1515 Quintara Street
San Francisco, CA 94116

Creekside Oaks Charter
Elementary School
2030 First Street
Lincoln, CA 95648

Crenshaw Learn Charter High
School
5010 11th Avenue
Los Angeles, CA 90043

Dayspring Institute Charter High
School
3355 E. Shields Avenue
Fresno, CA 93726

Deterding Charter Elementary
School
6000 Stanley Avenue
Carmichael, CA 95608

Discovery Charter School
1100 Camino Biscay
Chula Vista, CA 91991

East Palo Alto Charter School
1286 Runnymede Street
East Palo Alto, CA 94303

Edison-Bethune Charter Academy
16161 S. Fruit Street
Fresno, CA 93706

Edison Charter Academy
3531 22nd Street
San Francisco, CA 94114

Edison Elementary Charter
School
135 Van Ness Avenue
San Francisco, CA 94102

Edison Elementary Charter
School
2425 Kansas Avenue
Santa Monica, CA 90404

Eel River Charter School, The
P.O. Box 218
Covelo, CA 95428

Elk Grove Charter School
5900 Banford Drive
Sacramento, CA 95823

Escondido Charter High School
1845 East Valley Parkway
Escondido, CA 92027

Feasster-Edison Charter School,
The
670 Flower Street
Chula Vista, CA 91910

Fenton Avenue Charter School
11828 Gain Street
Lake View Terrace, CA 91342

Fifty-Fourth Street Charter
Elementary
5501 S. Eileen Avenue
Los Angeles, CA 90043

Fort Ross Charter School
520 Mendocino Avenue, #273
Santa Rosa, CA 95401

Forty-Second Street Charter
School
4231 Fourth Avenue
Los Angeles, CA 90008

Freshwater Charter Middle
School
75 Greenwood Heights Drive
Eureka, CA 95501

Garfield Charter School
3600 Middlefield Road
Menlo Park, CA 94025

Gates Charter Language School
23882 Landisview Avenue
Lake Forest, CA 92630

Gate Way Charter Academy
School
949 F Street
Fresno, CA 93706

George Washington
Charter School
45-768 Portola
Palm Desert, CA 92260

Gorman Charter School
49847 Gorman School Road
P.O. Box 104
Gorman, CA 93243

Grass Valley Charter School
235 South Auburn Street
Grass Valley, CA 95945

Grayson Charter School
P.O. Box 7
Westley, CA 95387

Grove Charter High School, The
1890 Orange Avenue
Redlands, CA 92373

Grove High School
200 Nevada
Redlands, CA 92373

Hart-Ransom Academic Charter
School
3920 Shoemake Avenue
Modesto, CA 95358

Hickman Charter School
13306 4th Street
P.O. Box 10
Hickman, CA 95323

Home Tech Charter School
6445 Skyway
Paradise, CA 95969

Hyde Park Charter School
3140 Hyde Park Boulevard
Los Angeles, CA 90043

Idyllwild Charter High School
P.O. Box 1817
Idyllwild, CA 92549

Indio Charter School
44-700 Palm Street
Indio, CA 99220

John C. Fremont Charter School
1120 W. 22nd Street
Merced, CA 95340

Julian Charter School
P.O. Box 1780
1704 Cape Horn Avenue
Julian, CA 92036

Kenter Canyon LEARN/Charter
School
645 N. Kenter Avenue
Los Angeles, CA 90049

Kenwood Charter School
2213 Mendocino Avenue
Santa Rosa, CA 95403

Keyes to Learning Charter School
P.O. Box 519
Keyes, CA 95328

Kid Street Learning Center
Charter School
54 West 6th Street
Santa Rosa, CA 95406

Kingsburg Community Charter
Extension (Home School)
1776 6th Avenue
Kingsburg, CA 93631

Kingsburg Elementary Charter
District
1310 Stroud Avenue
Kingsburg, CA 93631

Kwachiiyoa Charter School
6365 Lake Atlin Avenue
San Diego, CA 92119

Lammersville Charter School
16555 W. Von Sosten Road
Tracy, CA 95376

Language Acquisition Magnet
Program Charter School
Temecula, CA 92592

Learning Community
Charter School
1859 Bird Street
Oroville, CA 95965

Linscott Charter School
220 Elm Street
Watsonville, CA 95076

Louisiana Schnell Elementary
Charter School
Placerville Union Elementary
School District
Placerville, CA 95667

Lubeles Academy Charter School
85 Rose Avenue
Chico, CA 95928

Mare Island Technology Academy
611 Amador
Vallejo, CA 94591

Marlton Charter School
4000 Santo Tomas Drive
Los Angeles, CA 90008

Marquez Charter School
16821 Marquez Avenue
Pacific Palisades, CA 90272

Mattole Valley Charter School
P.O. Box 39
Honeydew, CA 95545

Memorial Academy Charter
2850 Logan Avenue
San Diego, CA 92113

Meroe International Academy
Charter School
P.O. Box 32386
Oakland, CA 94604

Mid-City Charter Magnet School
3100 W. Adams Boulevard
Los Angeles, CA 90018

Mid Valley Alternative Charter
School
9895 7th Avenue
Hartford, CA 93230

Modoc Charter School
1670 Market Street #268
Redding, CA 96001

Montague Charter Academy
13000 Montague Street
Pacoima, CA 91331

Mountain Home School Charter
P.O. Box 395
Oakhurst, CA 93644

Mueller Elementary Charter
School
715 I Street
Chula Vista, CA 91910

Muir Charter School
10031 Joerschke Drive, Suite D
Grass Valley, CA 95945

Napa Valley Charter School
P.O. Box 2367
Yountville, CA 94599

Natomas Charter School
3710 Del Paso Road
Sacramento, CA 95834

Nevada City Home Study
Charter School
215 Washington Street
Nevada City, CA 95959

New Hope Charter School
1420 S. Mills, Suite M
Lodi, CA 95242

New Jerusalem Charter School
31400 S. Koster Road
Tracy, CA 95376

New Millennium Institute of
Education Charter School
830 Fresno Street, Suite 400
Fresno, CA 93721

New Village Public Charter School
1086 Alcatraz Avenue
Oakland, CA 94608

Novato Charter School
601 Bolling Drive
Novato, CA 94949

Oakdale Charter School
1235 East D Street
Oakdale, CA 95361

Oakland Charter Academy
4703 Tidewater Avenue
Oakland, CA 94601

Oak Tree Charter School
1445 101st Avenue
Oakland, CA 94603

Odyssey Charter School
1555 E. Colorado Boulevard
Pasadena, CA 91106

Open Charter Magnet School, The
5540 West 77th Street
Los Angeles, CA 90045

Open Charter School, The
6085 Airdrome Street
Los Angeles, CA 90035

Opportunities for Learning
Charter School
180 S. Lake Avenue
Pasadena, CA 91101

Options for Youth—
Victor Valley Charter School
199 S. Los Robles Avenue,
Suite 700
Pasadena, CA 91101

Orange County Charter School
200 Kalmus Drive
Costa Mesa, CA 92626

Pacific Coast Charter School
292 Green Valley Road
Watsonville, CA 95076

Pacific Community Charter School
P.O. Box 1701
Santa Cruz, CA 95468

Pacific View Charter School
P.O. Box 269
Loleta, CA 95551

Pacific View Charter School
3355 Mission Avenue, Suite 139
Oceanside, CA 92054

Palisades Charter High School
15777 Bowdoin Street
Pacific Palisades, CA 90272

Palisades Elementary Charter
800 Via De La Paz
Pacific Palisades, CA 90272

Paradise Charter Middle School
6473 Clark Road
Paradise, CA 95969

Paradise Charter Network/
Independent Learning Center
645 Pearson Road
Paradise, CA 95969

Paul Revere Charter/
Learn Middle School
1450 Allenford Avenue
Los Angeles, CA 90049

Peobody Charter School
3018 Calle Noguera
Santa Barbara, CA 93105

Piner-Olivet Charter School
3450 Coffey Lane
Santa Rosa, CA 95470

Pioneer Union Elementary
Charter District
8810 14th Avenue
Hanford, CA 93230

Plumas Charter School
2288 East Main Street
Quincy, CA 95971

Prosser Creek Charter School
12640 Union Mills Road
Truckee, CA 96161

Ravenswood-Edison Charter
School
2033 Pulgas Avenue
East Palo Alto, CA 94303

Ready Springs Charter School
10862 Spenceville Road
Penn Valley, CA 95949

River Oak Public Charter School
555 Leslie Street
Ukiah, CA 95482

San Carlos Charter Learning
Center
750 Dartmouth Avenue
San Carlos, CA 94070

Sanger Hallmark Charter
1905 Seventh Street
Sanger, CA 93657

Santa Barbara Charter School
6100 Stow Canyon Road
Goleta, CA 93117

Santa Rosa Education
Cooperative Charter School
1835A W. Steele Lane
Santa Rosa, CA 95403-2628

Sebastopol Independent Charter
School
P.O. Box 1170
Sebastopol, CA 95473

Seventy-Fourth LEARN/Charter
School
2112 W. 74th Street
Los Angeles, CA 90047

Shearer Charter School
1590 Elm Street
Napa, CA 94559

Sheridan Charter School
4730 H Street
Sheridan, CA 95681

Sherman Oaks Community
Charter School
1800-C Fruitdale Avenue
San Jose, CA 95128

Sierra Charter School, The
2014 Tulare, Suite 718
Fresno, CA 93721

SLVUSD Charter School
6264B Highway 9
Felton, CA 95018

Soledad Enrichment Action
Charter Schools
3763 East 4th Street
Los Angeles, CA 90022

Sonoma Charter School
17202 Sonoma Highway
Sonoma, CA 95476

Sonoma County Charter School:
Petaluma Cooperative School
1000 Corona Road
Petaluma, CA 94954

South Bay Charter School
601 Elm Avenue
Imperial Beach, CA 91932

Stellar Charter School of
Technology
5885 E. Bonnyview Road
P.O. Box 99
Redding, CA 96099-2418

Sunset Charter School
1755 S. Crystal
Fresno, CA 93706

Topanga LEARN/Charter
Elementary School
141 N. Topanga Canyon Boulevard
Topanga, CA 90290

Twin Ridges Home
Study Charter School
P.O. Box 529
N. San Juan, CA 95960

Union Hill School District
Charter School
10879 Bartlett Drive
Grass Valley, CA 95945

View Park Preparatory
Accelerated Charter School
3751 West 54th Street
Los Angeles, CA 90043

Virginia Road Charter
Elementary School
2925 Virginia Road
Los Angeles, CA 90016

Visions in Education Home
Charter School
6939 Sunrise Boulevard, Suite 207
Citrus Heights, CA 95610

Vivian Banks Charter School
Pala Mission Road
Pala, CA 92059

Voyager Charter School—
Options for Youth
102 E. Broadway
San Gabriel, CA 91776

Washington Charter School
45-768 Portola Avenue
Palm Desert, CA 92260

W.E.B. DuBois Charter School
302 Fresno Street #205
Fresno, CA 93706

Western Avenue Charter School
1724 53rd Street
Los Angeles, CA 90062

West Park Charter Academy
2695 S. Valentine Avenue
Fresno, CA 93706

Westside Charter School
6537 W. 2nd Street
Rio Linda, CA 95673

West Sonoma Charter School
520 Mendocino Avenue, #225
Santa Rosa, CA 95401

Westwood Charter Elementary School
2050 Selby Avenue
Los Angeles, CA 90025-6311

Westwood Charter School
2700 Kilburn Avenue
Napa, CA 94558

Whitney Young LEARN Charter HS
3051 W. 52nd Street
Los Angeles, CA 90043

Willits Charter School
7 South Marin Street
Willits, CA 95490

Woodlands Charter School
3801 Low Gap Road
Ukiah, CA 95482

Yuba County Career Preparatory Charter School
938 14th Street
Marysville, CA 95901

Yuba River Charter School
P.O. Box 1725
Nevada City, CA 95959

Yucca Mesa Charter School
P.O. Box 1209
29 Palms, CA 92277

Colorado

Boulder Preparatory High School
2895 28th Street
Boulder, CO 80302

Classical Academy
8650 Scarborough Drive
Colorado Springs, CO 80920

Community Involved Charter School
7700 West Woodard Drive
Lakewood, CO 80227

Connect School, The
107 East 7th Street
Pueblo, CO 81002

Core Knowledge Charter School
10423 Parker Road
Parker, CO 80134

Littleton Prep Charter School
5151 South Federal Boulevard
Littleton, CO 80123

Odyssey Charter School
6430 Martin Luther King Boulevard
Denver, CO 80207

Pioneer Charter School
3230 East 38th Avenue
Denver, CO 80205

Pueblo School for the Arts and Sciences
1745 Acero
Pueblo, CO 81004

Connecticut

Amistad Academy
407 James Street
New Haven, CT 06513

Brooklawn Academy
108 Biro Ave
Fairfield, CT 06430

Odyssey Community School
440 Oakland Street
Manchester, CT 06040

Sport Sciences Academy
338 Asylum Street
Hartford, CT 06103

Delaware

Charter School of Wilmington, The
100 North DuPont Road
Wilmington, DE 19807

East Side Charter School
2401 Thatcher Street
Wilmington, DE 19802

Positive Outcomes Charter School
522 South State Street
Dover, DE 19901

Florida

Academie Da Vinci
1380 Pinehurst Road
Dunedin, FL 34698

Academy for Applied Training
350 Braden Avenue
Sarasotak, FL 34243

Academy of Environmental Science
12695 West Fort Island Trail
Crystal River, FL 34429

Alachua Learning Center
P.O. Box 1389 11100 SR 235
Alachua, FL 32616

Alee Academy
755 South Central Avenue
Umatilla, FL 32784

Beulah Academy of Science, Inc.
5805 Beulah Church Road
Pensacola, FL 32526

Campus Primary Developmental Research School, The
2929 Cheney Highway
Titusville, FL 32780

Challenge for Success School
2925 Optimist Drive
Marianna, FL 32448

Chance Charter School
209 NW 75th Street
Gainesville, FL 32607

Charter School of Excellence
1217 SE 3rd Avenue
Fort Lauderdale, FL 33316

Charter School of Tampa Bay Academy
12012 Boyette Road
Riverview, FL 33569

Child Development Center Charter School
716 E. Bella Vista Street
Lakeland, FL 33805

City of Pembroke Pines Charter Elementary Schools East Campus
10801 Pembroke Road
Pembroke Pines, FL

City of Pembroke Pines Charter Middle School
18500 Pembroke Road
Pembroke Pines, FL

Coral Reef Montessori
19000 SW 112 Avenue
Miami, FL 33257

Daniel Payne Academy
5258-3 Norwood Avenue
Jacksonville, FL 32208

Devon Charter School
500 Art Lane
Sanford, FL 32771

Dizzy Gillespie School
of the Fine & Performing Arts
3620 SE Dixie Highway
Stuart, FL 34997

Doral Academy, The
7700 NW 98th Street
Miami, FL 33016

Educational Horizons
3000 Fiske Boulevard
Rockledge, FL

Ed Venture Charter School
117 East Coast Avenue
Hypoluxo, FL 33462

Einstein Montessori School
5930 SW Archer Road
Gainesville, FL 32608

Empowering Young Minds
Academy
5564 Norwood Avenue
Jacksonville, FL 32208

Escambia Charter School, Inc.
P.O. Box 1147
Gonzalez-Pensacola, FL 32560

Explorer Elementary and
Middle School
9150 Ellis Road
Melbourne, FL 32940

Expressions Learning Arts
Academy
5408 SW 13th Street
Gainesville, FL 32608

Foundation School, The
1325 George Jenkins Boulevard
Lakeland, FL 33815

Frank Sqanga Charter School
310-B Douglas Street
New Smyrna Beach, FL 32168

Indian River Charter High School
6055 College Lane
Vero Beach, FL 32966

Joseph Littles-Nguzo
Saba Charter School
2105 N. Australian Avenue
West Palm Beach, FL 33407

Lake Eola Charter School
135 N. Magnolia Avenue
Orlando, FL 32802

Manatee School of Arts &
Sciences
7315 1st Avenue W
Brandenton, FL 34221

Mater Academy
7700 NW 103rd Street
Hialeah Gardens, FL 30160

McKeel Academy of Technology
1810 West Parker Street
Lakeland, FL 33815

Metropolitan Ministries Academy
2002 North Florida Avenue
Tampa, FL 33602

Miami Shores/Barry University Charter School
11441 NW Second Avenue
Miami Shores, FL 33168

Micanopy Area Cooperative School
P.O. Box 386
Micanopy, FL 32667

Montessori Elementary Charter School
1221 Valera Street
Key West, FL 33040

New Dimensions High School
4900 Pleasant Hill Road
Kissimmee, FL 34759

North Lauderdale Academy High School
7201 Kimberly Blvd
North Lauderdale, FL 33068

Odyssey Charter School
344 Emerson Drive NW
Palm Bay, FL 32907

Okaloosa Academy Charter School
81 Roberts Street
Ft. Walton Beach, FL 32547

One Room School House
1214 SE 4th Street
Gainesville, FL 32601

PAL Academy Charter Middle School
202 13th Avenue East
Bradenton, FL 34208

Palm Bay Academy
2145 Palm Bay Road NE
Palm Bay, FL 32905

Partnership Academy, The
101 NW Avenue C
Belle Glade, FL 33430

Passport School, Inc.
1890 Conway Gardens Road
Orlando, FL 32806

Princeton House Charter School
630 West Princeton Street
Orlando, FL 32804

Rader School of Santa Rosa County, The
4062 Avalon Boulevard
Milton, FL 32583

Rays of Hope Charter School
1660 West Airport Boulevard
Sanford, FL 32773

Renaissance School, The
6075 S. Florida Avenue
Lakeland, FL 33813

Renaissance Learning Center
4077 Holly Drive
Palm Beach Gardens, FL 33410

Richardson Academy, Inc., The
2150 W. Dr. Martin Luther King Jr. Boulevard
Tampa, FL 33607

Ryder System Charter School in the Workplace
3600 NW 82nd Avenue
Miami, FL 33166

Sarasota School of Arts and
Sciences
645 Central Avenue
Sarasota, FL 34236

School of Success Academy
(S.O.S.)
6974 Wilson Boulevard
Jacksonville, FL 32210

Sculptor Elementary School
P.O. Box 490
Sharpes, FL 32959

Seaside Neighborhood School
10 Smolian Circle
P.O. Box 4610
Seaside, FL 32459

Smart School Charter Middle
School
3698 NW 15th Street
Lauderhill, FL 33311

Somerset Academy, The
12425 SW 53rd Street
Miramar, FL 33027

Spiral Tech Elementary
12400 SW 72nd Street
Miami, FL 33183

Summit Charter School
441 S. Wymore Road
Maitland, FL 32751

Suncoast School for Innovative
Studies
P.O. Box 49644
1661 Main Street
Sarasota, FL 34230

Terrace Community School
6720 East Fowler Avenue
Temple Terrace, FL 33617

Trinity School For Children
6815 N. Rome
Tampa, FL 33604

University of South Florida
Charter School
HMS 401, USF
Tampa, FL 33620

Wakulla's Charter School of Arts,
Science, and Technology
(C.O.A.S.T.)
48 Shell Island Road
P.O. Box 338
St. Marks, FL 32355

Youth Co-op Charter School
12051 W. Okeechobee Road
Hieleah Gardens, FL 33018

Georgia

Addison Elementary School
3055 Ebenezer Road
Marietta, GA 30066

Cartersville Elementary School
340 Old Mill Road
Catersville, GA 30120

Stone Mountain chARTer School
6206 Memorial Drive
Stone Mountain, GA 30083

Hawaii

Connections Charter School
Highway 11
Mountain View, HI 96771

Innovations Public Charter School
76-147 Royal Poinciana Drive
Kailua-Kona, HI 96740

**Kanu o ka 'Aina New Century
Public Charter School**
Kamuela, HI 96743

Kihei High School
321 Hale Kai Street
Kihei, HI 96753

Lanikai School
140 Ala Road
Kailua, HI 96734

Waialae School
1045 19th Avenue
Honolulu, HI 96815

**West Hawaii Explorations
Academy—Public Charter School**
73-4460 Queen Ka'ahumanu
Highway, #105
Kailua-Kona, HI 96740

Idaho

Coeur d'Alene Charter Academy
711 West Kathleen Avenue
Coeur d'Alene, ID 83814

**Pocatello Community
Charter School**
P.O. Box 1092
Pocatello, ID 83204

Renaissance Charter School
106 N. Van Buren
Moscow, ID 83843

Teton Valley Charter School
Driggs, ID 83422

Illinois

ACORN Charter High School
3814 W. Iowa Avenue
Chicago, IL 60651

Alain Locke Charter Academy
123 N. Wacker Drive, #900
Chicago, IL 60606

**Betty Shabazz International
Charter School**
7825 Ellis Avenue
Chicago, IL 60619

**Chicago International Charter
School**
2235 N. Hamilton Avenue
Chicago, IL 60647

**Edison-Great Builders of Cities
Charter School**
1105 W. Lawrence Avenue
Chicago, IL 60640

**Galesburg Community Choice
Classroom**
1072 W. North Street
Galesburg, IL 61401

Golden Apple Charter School
8 S. Michigan Avenue, #700
Chicago, IL 60603

Noble Street Charter School
1012 Noble Street
Chicago, IL 60622

**North Kenwood/Oakland
Charter School**
4611 South Ellis Avenue
Chicago, IL 60653

**North Lawndale College Prep.
Charter High School**
1616 S. Spaulding Avenue
Chicago, IL 60653

Perspectives Charter School
1532 South Michigan Avenue
Chicago, IL 60605

**Triumphant Charter Middle
School**
4953 S. Seeley Street
Chicago, IL 60643

**YouthBuild Rockford Charter
School**
310 South Avon Street
Rockford, IL 61102

Kansas

**Basehor-Linwood Virtual
Charter School**
2108 N. 155th Street
Basehor, KS 66007

**Dodge City Academy Public
Charter School**
2000 6th Avenue
Dodge City, KS 67801

John Dewey Learning Academy
601 Woodson
Lecompton, KS 66050

Peoria Street Charter School
105 E. 5th Street, Box 550
Louisburg, KS 66053

Louisiana

**ACE (Academy and Career
Education) School**
Route 2, Box 112-C
Ville Platte, LA 70586

Bayou Charter School
c/o 319 Bayou Black Drive
Houma, LA 70360

Children's Charter School
900 McClung Avenue
Baton Rouge, LA 70802

**J.K. Haynes Elementary Charter
School**
356 East Boulevard
Baton Rouge, LA 70802

Lafayette Charter High School
516 E. Pinhook Road
Lafayette, LA 70501

**SABIS International Charter
School of Pine Grove**
St. Helena Parish
P.O. Box 101
Greenburg, LA 70760

**Street Academy Charter School,
The**
2524 Napoleon Avenue
New Orleans, LA 70115

**Virgil T. Browne Glencoe Charter
School**
4517 LA 83
Franklin, LA 70538

Massachusetts

**Academy of the Pacific Rim
Charter School**
1035 Beacon Street
Brookline, MA 02146

**Benjamin Banneker Charter
School**
21 Notre Dame Avenue
Cambridge, MA 02140

Boston Evening Academy Charter
School
41 Berkeley Street
Boston, MA 02116

Boston Renaissance Charter
School
250 Stuart Street
Boston, MA 02116

Cape Cod Lighthouse Charter
School
225 Route 6A, Box 1959
Orleans, MA 02653

City on a Hill Charter School
320 Huntington Avenue
Boston, MA 02115

Health Careers Academy Charter
School
360 Huntington Avenue
Boston, MA 02115

Lawrence Family Development
Charter School
34 West Street
Lawrence, MA 01841

Neighborhood House Charter
School
197A Centre Street
Dorchester, MA 02124

New Leadership Charter School
1170 Carew Street
Springfield, MA 01109

North Star Academy Charter
School
1259 E. Columbus Avenue
Springfield, MA 01103

Roxbury College Preparatory
Charter School
1575 Tremont Street
Roxbury, MA 02120

SABIS International Charter
School
120 Ashland Avenue
Springfield, MA 01103

Seven Hills Charter School
51 Cage Street
Worcester, MA 01605

Somerville Charter School
15 Webster Avenue
Somerville, MA 02143

South Boston Harbor Academy
Charter School
7 Elkins Street
Boston, MA 02127

Michigan

Academy for Business and
International Studies
26104 Eton Avenue
Dearborn Heights, MI 48125

Ann Arbor Learning Community
4220 Packard
Ann Arbor, MI 48108

Chandler Woods Charter Academy
Post Road
Belmont, MI 49306

Compass Charter Academy
13330 168th Street
Grand Haven, MI 49417

Countryside Charter School
4800 Meadowbrook Road
Benton Harbor, M1 49022

El-Hajj Malik El-Shabazz
Academy
2130 W. Holmes Street
Lansing, MI 48601

Excel Charter Academy
4201 Benton Road SE
Grand Rapids, MI 49512

Linden Charter Academy
3244 Linden Road
Flint, MI 48504

Michigan Institute for Construc-
tion Trades & Technology
P.O. Box 07472
Detroit, MI 48207

North Saginaw Charter Academy
Trautner Road
Saginaw, MI 48604

Ridge Park Charter Academy
2428 Burton Street SE
Grand Rapids, MI 49546

University Public School
2727 Second Avenue
Detroit, MI

Walton Charter Academy
744 East Walton Boulevard
Pontiac, MI 48340

Minnesota

Blufview Montessori School
354 Lafayette Street
Winona, MN 55987

Community of Peace Academy
471 Magnolia Avenue E
St. Paul, MN 55101

Concordia Creative Learning
Academy
1355 Pierce Butler Route
St. Paul, MN 55104

E.C.H.O. Charter School
301 First Street E
Echo, MN 56237

Eci' Nompa Woonspe' Charter
School
P.O. Box 10
280 N. Centennial Drive
Morton, MN 56270

Martin Hughes Charter School
P.O. Box 726
200 Wanless Street
Buhl, MN 55713

Odyssey Charter School
6510 Zane Avenue N
Brooklyn Park, MN 55429

Right Step Academy
245 East Sixth Street, Suite 255
St. Paul, MN 55101

St. Paul Family Learning Center
Charter School
1745 University Avenue West,
Suite 100
St. Paul, MN 55104-3624

T-M Charter School
7705 Western Avenue
Meadowlands, MN 55765

Twin Cities Academy Charter
School
486 View Street
St. Paul, MN 55102

Village School of Northfield
209 Oak Street
Northfield, MN 55057

Mississippi

Hayes Cooper Center for Math,
Science, & Technology
500 North Dr. Martin Luther King
Merigold, MS 38759

Missouri

Kansas City Foreign Language
Charter School, The
P.O. Box 10003
Kansas City, MO 64171

Southwest Charter School
Kansas City, MO

Urban Community Leadership
Academy
1524 The Paseo Boulevard
Kansas City, MO 64108

New Jersey

Academy Charter High School
1725 Main Street S
Belmar, NJ 07719

Alexander Hamilton Charter
School
P.O. Box 2283
Paterson, NJ 07509

CALLA Charter School
P.O. Box 1401
Plainfield, NJ 07061

Camden's Promise Charter School
879 Beideman Avenue
Camden, NJ 08105

ChARTer TECH HS for the
Performing Arts
390 Poplar Avenue
Linwood, NJ 08221

Family Alliance Charter School
117 Ridgewood Way
Burlington, NJ 08016

Franklin Charter School
3 Jimmy Court
Somerset, NJ 08873

Galloway Kindergarten Charter
School
Village Greene A1
615 E. Moss Mill
Absecon, NJ 08016

Greater Brunswick Charter School
P.O. Box 1389
Highland Park, NJ 08904

Hoboken Charter School
105 9th Street
Hoboken, NJ 07030

Newark Charter School
8 Chestnut Street
Princeton, NJ 08542

North Star Academy Charter
School of Newark
10 Washington Place
Newark, NJ 07102

Ocean City chARTer Tech HS
for Performing Arts
P.O. Box 241
Ocean City, NJ 07102

Red Bank Charter School
65 West Front Street
Red Bank, NJ 07701

New Mexico

Broad Horizons Educational
Center
1034 Community Way
Portales, NM 88130

Harrison Middle School
3912 Isleta Boulevard SW
Albuquerque, NM 87105

Highland High School
4700 Coal Avenue SE
Albuquerque, NM 87108

Taylor Middle School
Albuquerque, NM

Turquoise Trail Elementary
RR 16 Box 800
Sante Fe, NM 87505

New York

Encuentro Ethical Charter School
1708 Lexington Avenue
New York, NY 10029

New Covenant Charter School
Albany, New York

North Carolina

American Renaissance Charter
School
1670 E. Broad Street, Suite 128
Statesville, NC 28625

Arapahoe Charter School
P.O. Box 158
Arapahoe, NC 28510

Arts & Basics Charter School
ABC's
1006 F Street N
Wilkesboro, NC 28659

Bear Grass
200 Green Street, Suite 202
Williamston, NC 27892

Brevard Academy
P.O. Box 2375
Brevard, NC 28712

Bridges
230 Hawthorne Road
Elkin, NC 28621

Bright Horizons Charter Academy
118 B South Berkeley Boulevard
Goldsboro, NC 27534

Cabarrus County Charter School
660 Concord Parkway
Concord, NC 28027

Cape Lookout Marine Science
High School
1108 Bridges Street
Morehead City, NC 28577

Carter Community School
800 N. Mangum Street
Durham, NC 27701

Carter G. Woodson School
437 Gold Floss Street
Winston-Salem, NC 27102

**Carter G. Woodson School of
Challenge**
P.O. Box 4423
Winston-Salem, NC 27104

**Catawba Valley Academy for
Applied Learning**
P.O. Box 1708
Hickory, NC 28603

**Change for Youth Charter
Academy**
P.O. Box 10355
Goldsboro, NC 27532

**Charter Day School/Roger Bacon
Academy**
Leland, NC

Chatham Charter School
P.O. Box 245
Silver City, NC 27344

CIS Academy
P.O. Box 706
Lumberton, NC 28359

Community Charter School, The
926 Elizabeth Avenue
Charlotte, NC 28204

Crossnore Academy
P.O. Box 249
Crossnore, NC 28616

Developmental Day School
P.O. Box 361
Statesville, NC 28687

Dillard Academy
P.O. Box 1188
Goldsboro, NC 27580

Downtown Middle School
280 S. Liberty Street
Winston-Salem, NC 27101

East Wake Academy
P.O. Box 65
Zebulon, NC 27597

East Winston Primary School
P.O. Box 16734
Winston-Salem, NC 27115

Elizabeth Grinton Academy
1109 Cartpath Road
Wilkesboro, NC 28659

**Englemann School of Arts &
Sciences**
2952 N. Oxford Street
Claremont, NC 28610

Evergreen Community Charter
2 Westwood Place, 2nd Floor
Asheville, NC 28806

Exploris Middle School
207 E. Hargett Street
Raleigh, NC 27601

**Francine Delany New School for
Children**
P.O. Box 16161
Asheville, NC 28816

Franklin Academy
604 Franklin Street
Wake Forest, NC 27587

Grandfather Academy
P.O. Box 2260
Banner Elk, NC 28604

Harnett Early Childhood
P.O. Box 989
Dunn, NC 28335

Healthy Start Academy
515 Dowd Street
Durham, NC 27701

Highland Public Charter School
324 North Highland Street
Gastonia, NC 28053-1653

Hope Elementary School
1116 N. Blount Street
Raleigh, NC 27604

Imani Institute
201 N. Church Street
Greensboro, NC 27401

Interconnections Charter High
School
2421 Heartly Drive
Raleigh, NC 27615

Kennedy Charter Public School,
Inc.
P.O. Box 472527
Charlotte, NC 28247

Kestrel Heights School
1915 Chapel Hill Road
Durham, NC 27707

Lake Norman Charter School
P.O. Box 312
Hunterville, NC 28078

Laurinburg Charter School
P.O. Box 1575
Laurinburg, NC 28353

Lincoln Charter School
P.O. Box 205
Lincolnton, NC 28093

Magellon Charter School
9400 Forum Drive
Raleigh, NC 27615

MAST School
1405 Midland Road
Southern Pines, NC 28387

Maureen Joy Charter School
320 Belvin Avenue
Durham, NC 27704

New Century Charter School
P.O. Box 4373
Chapel Hill, NC 27515

Northeast Raleigh Charter
8112 Round Oak Road
Raleigh, NC 27616

Oma's Inc. Charter School
P.O. Box 9234
Fayetteville, NC 28311

Orange County Charter School
660 Cornelius Street
Hillsborough, NC 27278

Partnership Academy Charter
School
6 Oakside Court
Durham, NC 27703

PHASE Academy of Jacksonville
P.O. Box 7037
Jacksonville, NC 28540

Piedmont Community Charter
School
P.O. Box 3706
Gastonia, NC 28054

PreEminent
6711 Brookmeade Place
Raleigh, NC 27612

Provisions Academy
P.O. Box 706
Sanford, NC 27330

Quality Education Academy
5012-D Lansing Drive
Winston-Salem, NC 27105

Quest Academy
9308 Fairbanks Road
Raleigh, NC 27613

Right Step Academy
1601 Halifax Street
Greenville, NC 27834

River Mill Charter School
The River Mill
Saxapahaw, NC 27340

Sallie B. Howard School
2000 Lipscomb Road
Wilson, NC 27893

Summit Charter School
P.O. Box 1339
Cashiers, NC 28717

Vance Charter School
P.O. Drawer 19
Henderson, NC 27536

Village Charter School
630 Weaver Dairy Road
Chapel Hill, NC 27514

Ohio

Aurora Academy Elementary
School
541 Utah Street
Toledo, OH 43605

City Day Community School
Elementary
210 N. Main Street
Dayton, OH 45402

Eagle Heights Academy
Elementary
1833 Market Street
Youngston, OH 44507

Harmony Community Middle
School
7030 Reading Road, Suite 350 #E
Cincinnati, OH 45237

Hope Academy Brown Street
Campus
1044 Brown Street
Akron, OH 44301

Horizon Science Academy—
Cleveland

Horizon Science Academy—
Columbus

Ida B. Wells Community Academy
The Academic Site: 1104 Johnston
Street
P.O. Box 9187
Tallmadge Avenue
Akron, OH 44305-2414

Northwest Ohio Building Trades
Academy
803 Line City Road
Rossford, OH 43460

Riser Military Academy
P.O. Box 16142
Columbus, OH 43216

Summit Academy For Alternative Learners
864 East Market
Akron, OH 44305

Oregon

HomeSource-Bethel Family Technology & Resource Center
P.O. Box 40884
Eugene, OR 97404

Pennsylvania

Alliance Charter School, The
1821-39 Cecil B. Moore Avenue
Philadelphia, PA 19121

Architecture and Design Charter High School of Philadelphia
105 South 7th Street
Philadelphia, PA 19106

Center for Economics and Law Charter School
3020 Market Street
Philadelphia, PA 19151

Centre Learning Community Charter School
411 S. Burrowes Street
State College, PA 16801

Chester Charter School, The
2722 W 9th Street
Chester, PA 19013

Christopher Columbus Charter School
Two Penn Center Plaza, Suite 1100
Philadelphia, PA 19102

Creative Educational Concepts Charter School
315 Edwards Street
Chester, PA 19013

Environmental Charter School
Point Pleasant, PA

Eugenio Maria DeHostos Community Bilingual Charter School
2726 N. 6th Street
Philadelphia, PA 19133

Family Charter School
3512 Haverford Avenue
Philadelphia, PA 19104

Freire Charter School
Philadelphia, PA

Futureworks Charter School
Pittsburgh, PA

GECAC Charter School
641 E. 22nd Street
Erie, PA 16503

Imhotep Charter School
7500 Germantown Avenue
Philadelphia, PA 19119

Keystone Education Center Charter School
425 S. Good Hope Road
Greenville, PA 12126

La Academie
30 N. Ann Street
Lancaster, PA 17602

Laboratory Charter School
of Communications and
Language, The
5359 Lebanon Avenue
Philadelphia, PA 191131

Learning Community Charter
School
Philadelphia, PA

Lehigh Valley Charter High
School
P.O. Box 1323
Bethlehem, PA 18016

Manchester Academic Charter
School
1214 Liverpool Street
Pittsburgh, PA 15233

Math, Science, & Technology
Community Charter School
P.O. Box 21095
Philadelphia, PA 19114

Mosaica Academy Charter School
2400 Bristol Pike
Bethlehem, PA 19020

Multi-Cultural Academy Charter
School
4666-68 N. 15th Street
Philadelphia, PA 19140

Nittany Valley Charter School
State College
2131 Sandy Drive
State College, PA 16803

Northeast Charter School
110 Betty Street
Eynon, PA 18403

Northside Urban Pathways
Charter School
201 Wood Street
Pittsburgh, PA 15222

Pennsylvania High School of
Business and Technology
Oil City, PA

Philadelphia Academy Charter
School
Northeast Philadelphia
Philadelphia, PA

Philadelphia Community
Academy
2820 N. 4th Street
Philadelphia, PA 19113

Philadelphia Harambee Institute
of Science and Technology
Charter School
2251 N. 54th Street
Philadelphia, PA 19131

Philadelphia World
Communication Charter School
512-20 S. Broad Street
Philadelphia, PA 19146

Preparatory Charter School, The
1631 E. Passyunk Avenue
Philadelphia, PA 19148

Ridgeview Academy Inc. Charter
School
1005 Village Way
Latrobe, PA 15650

Souderton Charter School
Collaborative
Souderton, PA

SUSQ-Cyber Charter School
90 Lawton Lane
Milton, PA 17447

Sylvan Heights Science Charter
School
1101 Market Street
Harrisburg, PA 17103

Thurgood Marshall Academy
Charter School
P.O. Box 86018
Pittsburgh, PA 15221

Urban League of Pittsburgh
Charter School
327 Negley Avenue
Pittsburgh, PA 15206

Village Charter School of
Chester-Upland
18 E. 8th Street
Chester, PA 19013

West Oak Lane Charter School
7157-59 Stenton Avenue
Philadelphia, PA 19138

World Communications Charter
School
Philadelphia, PA

Wyoming Valley Academy
Wilkes-Barre, PA

Youth Build Philadelphia Charter
School
619 Catherine Street
Philadelphia, PA 19147

Rhode Island

Times 2 Charter School
155 Harrison Street
Providence, RI 02908

South Carolina

Charter Alternative School
122 Broad Street
P.O. Box 947
Bernettsville, SC 29512

Greenville Technical Charter
High School
P.O. Box 5616
Greenville, SC 29606

Harbor School for Arts and
Sciences
1273 N. Fraser Street
Georgetown, SC 29440

Lighthouse Charter School
Hilton Head, SC

LOOP: Lots of Opportunities
for Progress
615 Clayton Street
McCormick, SC 29835

Marlboro County Alternative
Charter School
P.O. Box 86
Clio, SC 29525

Meyer Center for Special Children
1132 Rutherford Road
Greenville, SC 29609

Phoenix Center, The
Highway 261 West
Manning, SC 29102

School for Success
6 Osprey Pond Court
Columbia, SC 29223

Texas

**Academy of Accelerated
Learning, Inc.**
10700 NW Freeway, Suite 210
Houston, TX 77092

Academy of Austin
20755 Greenfield
Southfield, TX 48075

Academy of Skills and Knowledge
225 Winchester
Tyler, TX 75701

Academy of Transitional Studies
2203 Baldwin Boulevard
Corpus Christi, TX 78405

All Saint's Academy (A.S.A.)
8415 W. Belfort, Suite 200
Houston, TX 77071

**American Academy of Excellence
Charter-Austin**
P.O. Box 4173
Beaumont, TX 77704

**American Academy of Excellence
Charter-Houston**
P.O. Box 4173
Beaumont, TX 77704

American Institute for Learning
422 Congress Avenue
Austin, TX 78701

**Amigos Por Vida-Friends for
Life Center**
24075 Underwood Boulevard,
Suite 268
Houston, TX 77030

Arlington Classics Academy
2707 Yorkfield Court
Arlington, TX 76001

Benji's Special Education Academy
2903 Jensen Drive
Houston, TX 77026

**Blessed Sacrament Academy
Charter High School**
1135 Mission Road
San Antonio, TX 78210

Brazos Valley
6955 Broach Road
Bryan, TX 78008

Bright Ideas Charter
2507 Central Freeway E
Wichita Falls, TX 76302

**Building Alternatives Charter
School**
6903 Sunbelt Drive S
San Antonio, TX 78218

Burnham Wood Charter School
7310 Bishop Flores
El Paso, TX 79912

Cage Elementary Charter School
4528 Leeland
Houston, TX 78218

Career Plus Learning Academy
1023 N. Pine Street, Suite 101
San Antonio, TX 78202

Carrington Academy
1125 Lawrence Drive
Houston, TX 77008

Cedar Ridge
P.O. Box 217
Lometa, TX 76853

Centripet II
907 Preston
Pasadena, TX 77503

**Charter School for Abused,
Neglected, and Emotionally
Disturbed Children**
P.O. Box 681183
Houston, TX 77268

Children First Academy of Dallas
9336 Cedar Run
Dallas, TX 77268

**Children First Academy of
Houston**
9336 Cedar Run
Dallas, TX 75227

Coastal Bend Youth City
P.O. Box 268
Driscoll, TX 78351

Crockett Elementary
2112 Crockett
Houston, TX 77077

Crystan Hills Prep Academy
813 N. Zang Boulevard
Dallas, TX 75208

Dallas Advantage
13332 Montiford Drive, #11302
Dallas, TX 75240

**Dallas Can! Academy Charter
School**
2601 Live Oak
Dallas, TX 75204

Dallas Community
9245 Wayne Street
Dallas, TX 75223

Dallas County Juvenile Justice
2600 Lone Star Drive
Dallas, TX 75212

Eagle Advantage School
P.O. Box 380039
Duncanville, TX 75138

Earth Excels! Academy
Stephenville, TX

**Eastpark Pre Charter Middle
School**
1306 Cowden Court
Missouri City, TX 77489

East Texas Charter High School
3131 Drenanburg Court
Katy, TX 77449

Eden Park Academy
512 W. Stassney, Suite 100
Austin, TX 78745

Emma L. Harrison Charter School
1020 Elm Avenue
Waco, TX 76705

Galleria-Area Charter School
Post Oak YMCA
1331 Augusta
Houston, TX 77057

Genesis/Pegasus Charter School
Dallas, TX

George I. Sanchez Charter School
Houston, TX

Girls and Boys Preparatory Academy
Houston, TX

Heritage Academy
Dallas, TX

Impact Charter School
14442 Fonmeadow
Houston, TX 77035

John H. Wood Jr. Charter School
620 E. Afton Oaks Boulevard
San Antonio, TX 78232

KIPP, Inc. Charter School
7120 Beechnut
Houston, TX 77074

Life Charter School of Oak Cliff
4400 S.R.L. Thornton Freeway
Dallas, TX 75224

Medical Center Charter School
1920 N. Braeswood
Houston, TX 77030

Nancy New Charter School
1414 W. San Antonio Street
New Braunfels, TX 78130

New Frontiers Charter School
4018 S. Presa
San Antonio, TX 78223

North Hills School, The
2117 Walnut Hill Lane
Irving, TX 75038

One-Stop Multiservice Charter School
P.O. Box 164
McAllen, TX 78501

Raven School, The
P.O. Box 515
New Waverly, TX 77358

Sky's The Limit Charter School
222 East Riverside Drive, #212
Austin, TX 78704

Star Charter School
14200 N. IH-35
Austin, TX 78728

Texas Empowerment Academy
Austin, TX

Texas Language Charter School
307 Willow Brook
Duncanville, TX 75116

Transformative Charter Academy
807 N. 8th Street
Killeen, TX 76541

Treetops Schools International
D/FW Airport, TX

University Charter School
Box 7700
Austin, TX 78713

Valley High Charter School
514 South E. Street
Harlingen, TX 78550

Waco Charter School
615 N. 25th Street
Waco, TX 76707

West Houston Charter School
14333 Fern Avenue
Houston, TX 77079

Wyndam Charter School
11209 Clematis Lane
Houston, TX 77251

**YMCA of the Greater Houston
Charter School**
5614 H. Mark Crosswell
Houston, TX 77021

Utah

Jean Massieu School
Salt Lake City, UT

**Tuacahn High School for the
Performing Arts**
1100 Tuacahn Drive
Ivins, UT 84738

Virginia

Blue Ridge Technical Academy
Roanoke Higher Education Center
Roanoke, VA 24012

Washington, D.C.

**Integrated Design Electronics
Academy (IDEA) Public Charter
School**
1027 45th Street NE
Washington, D.C. 20019

Meridian Public Charter School
1328 Florida Avenue NW
Washington, D.C. 20009

**SEED Public Charter (Residential)
School of Washington, D.C.**
800 Third Street NE
Washington, D.C. 20002

**Techworld Public Charter
School, The**
Waterside Mall
401 M Street SW, Room 2718
Washington, D.C. 20024

**Washington Math Science
Technology**
Public Charter High School
401 M Street SW
Washington, D.C. 20024

**World Public Charter School of
Washington**
Casa Italiana
595-1/2 3rd Street NE
Washington, D.C. 20002

**Young Technocrats Science,
Technology, Public Charter
School, The**
Langley Junior High School
101 T Street NE
Washington, D.C. 20002

Wisconsin

Affiliated Alternatives
Madison, WI

Beaver Dam Charter School
400 E. Burnett Street
Beaver Dam, WI 53916

Chrysalis Family Charter School
1900 W. Tenth Avenue
Antigo, WI 54409

Core Knowledge Charter School
5890 Lacy Road
Fitchburg, WI 53711

Coulee Montessori Charter
School, La Crosse
901 Caledonia Street
La Crosse, WI 54603

Deerfield Charter High School
300 Simonson Boulevard
Deerfield, WI 53531

Glidden Charter School
370 S. Grant Street
Glidden, WI 54527

Leadership Academy Charter
School
2899 Highway 47
Lac du Flambeau, WI 54538

Lucas Charter School
N5630 200th Street
Menomonie, WI 54751

Mauston Alternative Resource
School (MARS)
Mauston, WI

McKinley Charter School
166 McKinley Road
Eau Claire, WI 54703

Monroe Alternative Charter
School
1220 16th Avenue
Monroe, WI 53566

Nature and Technology Charter
School
801 Second Avenue
P.O. Box 1517
Woodruff, WI 54568

Paideia Charter School Academy
5821 10th Ave
Kenosha, WI 53240

Rock River Charter School
527 S. Franklin Street
Janesville, WI 53545

T.E.A.M.S. Charter School
1201 N. Point Drive
Stevens Point, WI 54481

Waupaca County Charter School
160 N. Washington Street
Iola, WI 54945

Charter Schools in Development

Following is an additional list of charter schools scheduled to open in the
2000–2001 school year.

Arizona

Amerischools/Children's
   Academy (K–6), Phoenix

Arizona College Prep
   Academy (7–12), Phoenix

Mountain Rose Academy, Inc.,
   Tucson

California

Albert Einstein School,
   Yolo County

Blue Mountain Wilderness
Program, Camp

California Academy for Liberal
Studies, Los Angeles

California Hope Charter School,
Corona

Camino Nuevo Charter Academy,
Los Angeles

Career Advancement and
Technology Charter School,
Winton

Country Springs Elementary
School, Chino Hills

East Utica Charter School, Utica

Harmony Charter School,
San Joaquin

Knowledge Is Power Tech Institute,
Oakland

Merced Academy Charter School,
Merced

Pacific Grove Elementary School,
Garden Grove

Pembroke Pines Charter Middle
School, Pembroke Pines

Pomona Valley Y.E.S., Pomona

Semillas del Pueblo Charter School,
Los Angeles

Tehachapi Learning Center,
Tehachapi

University of Southern California
Prep School, Los Angeles

Canada

Charter School of Commerce,
Calgary

Colorado

A.C.E. Charter School, Colorado
Springs

Canyon West Academy, Arvada

Connecticut

Trailblazers Academy, Stamford

Florida

Museum Academy of Excellence,
Fort Lauderdale

Neighborhood Primary School,
The, Sharpes

Pensacola Academy for Success,
Pensacola

Stratford Educational Institute,
Edgewater

Techworld Public Charter School
of Miami, Miami

Georgia

Challenger Foundation, Acworth

Chamblee High School, Chamblee

Chamblee Middle School,
Chamblee

Charter Conservatory for Liberal
Arts & Tech, Statesboro

Cherokee Charter, Canton

Wagner Preparatory School, The,
Atlanta

Hawaii

Hawaii Academy of Arts &
Science, Pahoa

Illinois

Great American Adventure Club,
Centrailia

Maryland

Silver Spring Academy, Silver
Spring

Michigan

Advance Employment Services,
Lansing

South Arbor Charter Academy,
Ann Arbor

Minnesota

Voyageur Academy, Wadena

Missouri

International Baccalaureate Net
School, Kansas City

New Jersey

Proposed Capital City Charter
School, The, Trenton

New York

Academy for 21st Century Leaders
and Entrepreneurs, New York
City

Bright Future Elementary
Academy, Brooklyn

Multicultural Exchange Elementary
School, The Bronx

Seneca Charter School,
Irving

North Carolina

Charis International Charter
School, Asheville

Pennsylvania

H.T.L., Clariton

Texas

An Alternative-Residential
Charter School, Splendora

Big Spring Academy, Hunt

Utah

Murray Charter School, Murray

Virginia

Prince William Academy, Prince
William

Washington, D.C.

Media Technology & Social
Research Academy, Washington,
D.C.

Wisconsin

Pleasant River Schoolhouse,
Sauk City

BIBLIOGRAPHY

Bierlein, L.A., & L. Mulholland. (1993). *Charter School Up-date: Expansion of a Viable Reform Initiative.* Tempe: Arizona State University, School of Public Affairs.

Delpit, Lisa D. (1995). *Other People's Children: Cultural Conflict in the Classroom.* New York: The New Press.

Finn, C. E. Jr., B. V. Manno, L. A. Bierlein, & G. Vanourek. (1997). *Charter Schools in Action.* Indianapolis: The Hudson Institute.

Guide for charter school applicants. The New York Charter School Resource Guide (Charter School Resource Center), 41 Robbins Avenue, Amityville, New York 11701.

Hirsch, E. D., Jr. (1988). *Cultural Literacy.* Boston: Hougton-Mifflin.

———. (1998). *Core Knowledge Sequence.* Charlottesville, VA: Core Knowledge Foundation.

Hoff, David J. (2000). A teaching style that adds up. *Teacher Magazine,* February 23.

Oosterhof, A. (1999). *Developing and Using Classroom Assessments.* Upper Saddle River, NJ: Prentice Hall.

Perrone, Vito. (1991). *A Letter to Teachers.* San Francisco: Jossey Bass.

Popham, James W. (1999) *Testing! Testing! What Every Parent Should Know About School Tests.* Needham Heights, MA: Allyn and Bacon.

Principals quit New York City at a record pace. (1999). *New York Times,* September 30, A1, B6.

Pritchard, Ivor. (1998). *Good Education: The Virtues of Learning.* Judd Publishing.

Sarason, Seymour B. (1998). *Charter Schools, Another Flawed Educational Reform.* New York: Teachers College Press.

Steinberg, Laurence, B. Bradford Brown, and Sanford M. Dornbusch. (1997). *Beyond the Classroom: Why School Reform Has Failed and What Parents Need to Do.* New York: Simon and Schuster.

————. (1999). *National Study of Charter Schools.* Washington, D.C.: U.S. Department of Education.

————. (2000). *National Study of Charter Schools.* Washington, D.C.: U.S. Department of Education.

Vergari, Sandra. (1999, August 4). The challenges of oversight in a deregulated system. *Education and Urban Society* 31(4): 406–428.

Viteritti, Joseph P. (2000, February 23). School choice: Beyond the numbers. *Education Week* 19(24): 38, 44.

Watkins, Tom. (1995). *Education Digest* 65(6).

INDEX

ABOUT THE AUTHOR

FREDERICK A. BIRKETT, ED.M., a graduate of Harvard University's Graduate School of Education, has served as the executive director of two charter schools in the Boston area. He has performed consultant work for the New York State Charter School Resource Center, as well as provided consulting services and advice to organizations opening charter schools across the United States. He has spoken about charter schools at educational conferences up and down the Eastern Seaboard. For two years he served as the assistant headmaster of the Boston Renaissance Charter School. At present, Mr. Birkett is the executive director of the Benjamin Banneker Charter School in Cambridge, Massachusetts. He lives with his family in Medford, Massachusetts.